RUSSIAN REGIONAL

**CLASSIC DISHES FROM MOSCOW
AND ST. PETERSBURG; THE RUSSIAN FEDERATION
AND MOLDOVA; THE BALTIC STATES; GEORGIA,
ARMENIA, AND AZERBAIJAN; AND CENTRAL ASIA
AND KAZAKHSTAN**

RUSSIAN REGIONAL RECIPES

**CLASSIC DISHES FROM MOSCOW
AND ST. PETERSBURG; THE RUSSIAN FEDERATION
AND MOLDOVA; THE BALTIC STATES; GEORGIA,
ARMENIA, AND AZERBAIJAN; AND CENTRAL ASIA
AND KAZAKHSTAN**

SUSAN WARD

HACKBERRY PRESS

A QUANTUM BOOK

Published by
Hackberry Press, a division of The Texas Bookman
2700 Lone Star Drive
Dallas
Texas 75212
USA

Copyright ©MCMXCIII
Quintet Publishing Ltd.

This edition printed 2003

ISBN 1-931040-24-9

QUMTRR

This book is produced by
Quantum Publishing Ltd
6 Blundell Street
London N7 9BH

Typeset in Great Britain by
The Design Revolution
Manufactured in Singapore by
Eray Scan (Pte) Ltd.
Printed in Singapore by
Star Standard Industries (Pte) Ltd.

CONTENTS

UKRAINE

AREA: 603,700 SQ KMS
POPULATION: 51,704,000
CAPITAL: KIEV
MAIN LANGUAGES:
UKRAINIAN, RUSSIAN
RELIGION: ORTHODOX,
GREEK CATHOLIC

◆◆◆

ESTONIA

AREA: 45,000 SQ KMS
POPULATION: 1,573,000
CAPITAL: TALLINN
MAIN LANGUAGE: ESTONIAN
RELIGION: PROTESTANT

◆◆◆

LATVIA

AREA: 63,700 SQ KMS
POPULATION: 2,681,000
CAPITAL: RIGA
MAIN LANGUAGE: LATVIAN
(LETTISH)
RELIGION: PROTESTANT

◆◆◆

LITHUANIA

AREA: 65,200 SQ KMS
POPULATION: 3,690,000
CAPITAL: VILNIUS
MAIN LANGUAGE:
LITHUANIAN
RELIGION: ROMAN CATHOLIC

◆◆◆

MOLDOVA

AREA: 33,700 SQ KMS
POPULATION: 4,341,000
CAPITAL: KISHINEV
MAIN LANGUAGE:
ROMANIAN
RELIGION: ORTHODOX

◆◆◆

TURKMENISTAN

AREA: 488,100 SQ KMS
POPULATION: 3,534,000
CAPITAL: ASHKHABAD
MAIN LANGUAGE: TURKMEN
RELIGION: ISLAM

◆◆◆

ARMENIA

AREA: 29,800 SQ KMS
POPULATION: 3,283,000
CAPITAL: YEREVAN
MAIN LANGUAGE:
ARMENIAN
RELIGION: ORTHODOX

◆◆◆

GEORGIA

AREA: 69,700 SQ KMS
POPULATION: 5,449,000
CAPITAL: TBILISI
MAIN LANGUAGE:
GEORGIAN
RELIGION: ORTHODOX

◆◆◆

ESTONIA   ST. PETERSBURG

LATVIA

LITHUANIA

BELORUSSIA   MOSCOW

UKRAINE

MOLDOVA

GEORGIA

ARMENIA   AZERBAIJAN

TURKMENISTAN   UZBE

BELORUSSIA

AREA: 207,600 KMS
POPULATION: 10,200,000
CAPITAL: MINSK
MAIN LANGUAGE: BELORUSSIAN
RELIGION: ORTHODOX, ROMAN CATHOLIC

◆ ◆ ◆

AZERBAIJAN

AREA: 86,600 SQ KMS
POPULATION: 7,029,000
CAPITAL: BAKU
MAIN LANGUAGE: AZERI
RELIGION: ISLAM

◆ ◆ ◆

KAZAKHSTAN

AREA: 2,717,300 SQ KMS
POPULATION: 16,538,000
CAPITAL: ALMA-ATA
MAIN LANGUAGES: KAZAKH, RUSSIAN
RELIGION: ISLAM

◆ ◆ ◆

THE RUSSIAN FEDERATION

RUSSIAN FEDERATION

AREA: 17,075,400 SQ KMS
POPULATION: 147,386,000
CAPITAL: MOSCOW
MAIN LANGUAGE: RUSSIAN
RELIGION: ORTHODOX, ISLAM

◆ ◆ ◆

UZBEKISTAN

AREA: 447,400 SQ KMS
POPULATION: 19,906,000
CAPITAL: TASHKENT
MAIN LANGUAGE: UZBEK
RELIGION: ISLAM

◆ ◆ ◆

KAZAKHSTAN

KYRGYZSTAN

AREA: 198,500 SQ KMS
POPULATION: 4,291,000
CAPITAL: BISHKEK
MAIN LANGUAGE: KYRGYZ
RELIGION: ISLAM

◆ ◆ ◆

N   KYRGZSTAN

KISTAN

TAJIKISTAN

AREA: 143,100 SQ KMS
POPULATION: 5,112,000
CAPITAL: DUSHANBE
MAIN LANGUAGE: TAJIK
RELIGION: ISLAM

◆ ◆ ◆

INTRODUCTION

'DOBRO POZHALOVAT' – 'WELCOME AND GOODWILL'. THERE CAN BE NO BETTER INVITATION TO THESE PAGES THAN THE TRADITIONAL GREETING TO ANY VISITOR CROSSING THE THRESHOLD OF A RUSSIAN HOME. FOR THE RUSSIANS – INDEED ALL THE PEOPLES OF THE OLD RUSSIAN EMPIRE – ARE INTENSELY HOSPITABLE, A TRAIT FOSTERED BY BOTH GEOGRAPHY AND RELIGION. OUTSIDE THE CITIES, DISTANCES ARE GREAT, AND OFTEN MADE MORE DAUNTING BY INCLEMENT WEATHER, WHETHER THE ICE OF WINTER OR THE BEATING SUN OF SUMMER. IN SUCH PARTS OF THE WORLD TRAVELLERS TEND TO BE GIVEN SUCCOUR WITH A GENEROSITY UNKNOWN IN TAMER AND MORE POPULOUS REGIONS. AT THE SAME TIME, THE ORTHODOX CHURCH – WHICH HOLDS SWAY OVER THE MAJORITY OF THE OLD REPUBLICS – EMPHASIZES HOME AND CHRISTIAN FRIENDSHIP AS UNIFYING FACTORS IN THE COMMUNITY. THE MUSLIM CODE, AN IMPORTANT INFLUENCE IN SIX OF THE ASIAN REPUBLICS, PLACES SIMILAR IMPORTANCE ON HOME, HEARTH AND HOSPITALITY.

Until the 20th century, traditional Russian hospitality was firmly anchored within the class system; there was no clarion call to break the bonds of social caste when entertaining. That had to wait until the ascent of Lenin – a man whose idea of a party was inevitably prefaced by the word 'political'.

Given these social strictures, however, both peasants and patricians extended not only the warm hand of friendship to their visitors, but as much food and drink as they could manage. The staples of the poorest peasant were bread and salt (*khleb i sol*); these were elevated to the position of customary twin offerings accompanying the words of welcome. Even today, they are presented to guests at public receptions, at private family gatherings, and at the traditional *Maslenitsa* celebrations to welcome the advent of spring. Thus the hospitality of the lowest spread to the highest.

Conversely, the tradition of serving *zakuski* (singular, *zakuska*) – a table of 'small bites' – derived from the wealthy. It filtered down the social scale and throughout the Empire until it is now a fixture everywhere within the old Soviet sphere of influence, from the Baltic States to Caucasia and Central Asia.

The custom is thought to have originated on Chekhovian country estates outside Moscow, where long-distance visitors were greeted by an oval table groaning under a tantalizing array of pickles, vegetable salads, caviar, cured and creamed fish fillets, cold meats and pâtés, to be accompanied by warming shots of crystal-clear vodka. A substantial way of emphasizing the welcome initiated by the bread and salt, it was a kind of 'happy hour' guaranteed to callers who dropped in any time from late afternoon to the dinner hour. In the early 20th century hot dishes were added and, later, *zakuski* became firmly anchored to

A highly polished samovar has centre stage in the tea-time ritual of Mother Paisia, who has lived at the Phyti Russian Orthodox convent in Estonia for over 50 years.

NA ZDOROVYE – CHEERS!

Drinking in Russia and her neighbours is a serious business – whether it is alcoholically based or not! One of the most popular images in the Western mind is that of the great silver samovar dominating a table laden with Russian cakes and pastries. It is still a fixture of much Russian entertaining, though it is more often found in brass or stainless steel and is now electric, rather than heated by the charcoal-filled interior tube found in antique versions. On the top of the samovar sits a kettle with a strong brew of black tea. Hot water heated inside the samovar itself is drawn off by a spigot located at its lower front and is used to dilute the dark, bitter tea in the kettle. The tea is then poured into tall glasses with metal holders, and garnished with thin slices of lemon. In parts of Caucasia and in Central Asia and Kazakhstan, green tea is preferred.

This technique of brewing, as well as the dried black leaves of the tea plant, was brought back to the Russian capital in the 17th century by the tsar's first explorer-ambassador to China and Mongolia, yet the heavily tannic beverage did not become well known until the reign of Catherine the Great in the 18th century. In the 19th century the habit of tea-drinking spread from the landed gentry with their country tea parties to the urban bourgeoisie, and then to the masses.

Like tea, vodka ('little water') was initially the prerogative of the wealthy. Originally distilled from grape mashings, then rye, it was only in the mid-18th century that vodka began to be made from the imported potato. The folk mythology of the hard-drinking Russian was well-founded in fact; by that time the duties on salt and spirits were responsible for 30 per cent of the government's total tax revenue. In the days of the tsars, drinking vodka could thus be regarded as a form of patriotism!

Today, the best vodka is made from wheat and is distilled many times over. It should be drunk very chilled, in one gulp from a small glass, being preceded by a *zakuska* or at least a bite of black bread or a pickle to prepare the stomach. The ritual is then repeated again and again, until the appetite and the honour of the company is satisfied. The best unflavoured vodkas are Pschenichnaya, Stolichnaya (slightly sweetened) and Moskovskaya (with a small fizz of sodium bicarbonate); flavoured varieties include Zubrovka (a Polish bison-grass vodka), Pertsovka (a zippy pepper version), Okhotnichya (Hunter's vodka, with spices and herbs) and Limonnaya (a lemon-flavoured variety).

While good European-style lager (*pivo*) is only usually available in hotels and hard currency shops (*beryoska*), mildly alcoholic near-beer (*kvas*), is sold on Russian streets during warm weather. The commercial version is fermented from a combination of wheat, rye, buckwheat, water and sugar, and is sold in portable barrels wheeled around the city streets. They can be identified by the letters KBAC (*kvas*) stamped on the sides.

Most of the wines (*vino*) available in the CIS and Baltic States come from Georgia, Moldova and the Crimea. Both robust reds and whites are produced in Georgia, though they can often be unpalatably sweet for Western tastes. Moldova produces light, fruity whites, while much of the CIS champagne comes from the Crimea. A surprisingly acceptable brandy (*konyak*) is a speciality of Armenia and, to a lesser extent, Azerbaijan.

dinner itself, a marriage between Western cocktails and canapes and a traditional first course.

Of course the lavishness of the spread was – and is – always dictated by the economic circumstances of the host, but the emphasis is on plenty. It is also on variety, and it was on the *zakuska* table that some of the earliest introductions from the southern republics made their appearance in the north: steak tartare (*Myaso po-Tatarsky*), lamb kebabs (*shashlyk*), savoury fruit compotes and pickled watermelon, stuffed vegetables such as peppers, aubergines and vine leaves, and vegetable caviars – the most common being made from aubergines (*baklazhannayia ikra*). The idea was soon adapted to local mushrooms and even to the ubiquitous beetroot.

In return, Russian-style *zakuski* are found today in the farthest reaches of the old Soviet Union – even if they sometimes seem oddly out of place. The widespread use of sour cream made from cow's milk (*smetana*) in the European states is replaced by *matsoni* in Georgia, *matsun* in Armenia, *katyk* in Azerbaijan and *egurt* in Turkmenistan, all made with ewe's milk.

Ironically, the liberating transformation of the Union of Soviet Socialist Republics into the Commonwealth of Independent States – with the attendant non-participating states of Estonia, Latvia, Lithuania and Georgia – has come at a time when culinary cross-fertilization has never been greater. While the members and non-members of the CIS eye one another suspiciously, attempting to assert as much local sovereignty as possible, restaurants like the Baku (Azerbaijani cooking), the U Pirosmani and Zaydi-Poprobuy (Georgian cooking), and the Ko-op Kafe Yakimanka (Uzbek cooking) are among the most popular in Moscow. It is somehow less surprising that decent Swedish, Italian, Indian, Arabian and Tex-Mex restaurants, as well as the biggest McDonald's in the world, have all recently opened their doors in the capital. Ideology has demonstrably no place in the kitchen or at table in the new CIS.

Such gastronomic *glasnost* (openness) is to be welcomed, but warily. Most of the old state restaurants have always borne appalling reputations and the competition of the newer co-operative operations will raise standards eventually, benefiting visitors and citizens alike, but the opportunity for exploitation is rife. There is a fascination with anything western and an eagerness to attract foreign investment; corruption and scarcities bedevil the struggling supply infrastructure; and for over half a century the population has been starved of balanced historical perspective and creative inspiration. These combined factors are calculated to distort the present search for

Kvas (right) *is a traditional Russian drink made from pulled rye bread and honey, and fermented with yeast and sugar.* **Medok (left)** *combines kvas extract and honey, jam and fruit juice, while the middle drink is a concoction of honey and cranberries, with wine added to improve the taste and aroma.*

cultural – here specifically culinary – pride. Salvation must lie with that fabled and inherent hospitality which will brave queues, shortages and high prices, as well as resorting to bribery, to guarantee the best for guests. This desire to give pleasure, and to present the beloved Mother Country in the best possible light, is the most reliable indication that a return to pre-revolutionary food and traditions is a realizable ambition.

Russian Regional Recipes is both a celebration of things as they were and an anticipation of a renaissance already in its first stages. The collection of recipes on the following pages is composed of classics offered in ethnic Russian restaurants; of lesser-known regional dishes found in local homes and among immigrant communities abroad; and of interpretations of some historical recipes, making idiosyncratic ingredients and methods more acceptable to contemporary tastes.

The people of the Russian Federation and her neighbouring states are famously sentimental. Emigrés in the West speak with longing of their lost countries, and are returning there in growing numbers, despite the personal cost.

Perhaps this cookbook can give some slight flavour of what they left behind – and what they hope to find in their reclaimed future.

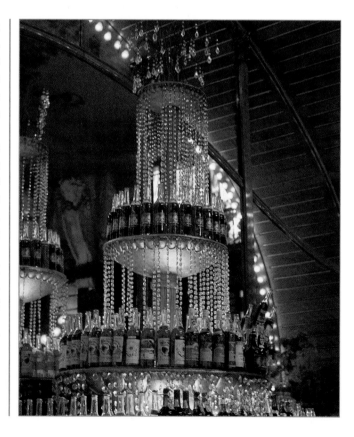

Gastronom No. 1, St Petersburg's most famous food hall, recalls the aristocratic opulence that could be found in Tsarist Russia.

THE RUSSIAN WAY OF EATING

BREAKFAST (*zavtrak*) is served late in hotels – usually between 8.00 and 10.00am. It can be even later in a private home – more like Western brunch, ending at 1.00pm. However, Western ways are ensuring that in urban centres, breakfast is becoming an earlier, rather than later, occasion.

In European 'Russia', it usually consists of tea, accompanied by sweet buns, rolls, bread and butter, curd cheese (*tvorog*) and/or buckwheat porridge and buttermilk. In hotels in Moscow, St Petersburg and other large cities, it may include other Western preferences such as fried or boiled eggs, cold cuts, fruit juice and watery instant coffee, as well as more elaborate ethnic dishes such as curd cheese pancakes (*tvorozhniki*) or curd cheese fritters (*syrniki*). If breakfast were taken very early – for instance on a farm – it might be followed by a second *zavtrak*.

LUNCH/DINNER (*obed*) has traditionally been the most important meal of the day, although that too is changing with the influence of Western culture and Western-style working conditions. A selection of *zakuski* – varying in elaborateness depending on whether it is a weekend or workday, a festive occasion or a family meal – may be followed by the option of soup, then a meat, fish or poultry course, ice cream, pudding or pastry, and coffee.

Lunch is a highly moveable feast, occurring any time from about 1.00 to 5.00pm. A weekend gathering or an important business lunch may linger for hours. If a second breakfast has been eaten, *obed* follows in the late afternoon.

TEA (*chai*) is a particularly unpredictable repast. During imperial times, afternoon or evening tea (*vecherny chai*) was a social imperative among the aristocracy and bourgeoisie, the later version a complement to the afternoon *zakuska* table. Cold cuts, cheese, cakes, pastries and biscuits, sweetmeats and candied fruits would be accompanied by tea and cordials.

Today one is less likely to encounter afternoon tea, though it is occasionally served in Moscow and central Russia. Afternoon coffee and cakes in the Baltic region are more of an institution. Tea in the Levantine manner – taken lingeringly at any time in the afternoon at a teahouse (*chaikhana*) – is the custom in Azerbaijan, Central Asia and Kazakhstan.

SUPPER (*ouzhin*) is yet another meal about which it is difficult to be precise. If two breakfasts and a late lunch were the order of the day, then supper would be very light or non-existent. Usually, however, supper can be any time from 7.00 to 10.00pm and takes the form of a lighter *obed* with fewer *zakuski*, or perhaps just a soup, a main course, dessert and no coffee.

On the other hand, late evening is often the time when city dwellers like to kick up their heels – in which case 'supper' can go on until well after midnight, and consists mostly of a succession of *zakuski* accompanied by enormous quantities of vodka. The idea is not so much to have a meal as to have an uproarious time and become extraordinarily drunk!

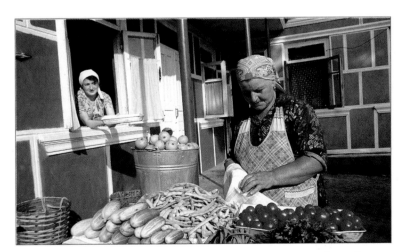

In the village of Makhvilauri, in south-western Georgia, a mother and daughter survey the harvest from their kitchen garden.

HERBS AND SPICES IN REGIONAL CUISINE

ALLSPICE (*pimient*)

The dried berries of the Jamaican pimento tree, combining the flavours of cinnamon, cloves and nutmeg, with perhaps a hint of pepper. Scandinavia is the world's major importer, followed closely by Russia and the western republics, which use large quantities in fish packing as well as in desserts, pastries and savoury dishes.

BASIL (*bazilik*)

Both the purple and green varieties are used in Caucasian cooking, giving a depth of flavour to meat dishes, marinades and salads.

CARAWAY (*t'meen*)

A relative of dill and fennel. The seeds are used to flavour pickles, fish, cabbage, sauerkraut, soup, pork dishes and some pastries.

CARDAMOM (*cardamon*)

The pods and seeds are used in international cooking; the seeds only are included in Russian, Balkan and Ukrainian pastries and pickles.

CINNAMON (*koritsa*)

True cinnamon is a native of Sri Lanka, the bark of the *Cinnamomum* tree, though the more bitter bark of Chinese species also goes by the name. It came to European Russia and the Baltic by way of the Levant and the southern empire and is much used in pastries and desserts.

CORIANDER (*koriandr*)

A herb which resembles flat-leaved parsley and is sometimes used interchangeably with it in Georgian and Armenian recipes, though it has a more dominant, pungent taste. Sprigs can be frozen or preserved in salt and oil, but do not dry successfully.

DILL (*ukrop*)

A popular herb in most East European and Scandinavian cookery. The seeds and, especially, the feathery leaves, have a distinctive sweet-sour flavour much liked for pickles, fish dishes and breads. Chopped dill leaves are also used as a garnish, for example for potatoes or sour cream.

GARLIC (*chesnock*)

Evidence suggests that this herb originated in Kirgizstan, and was brought to the northern Russian states by way of the Silk Road. It is much used in pickles and meat stews.

MARJORAM (*majoran*)

Used in Middle Eastern cooking, this herb has crept across the borders into savoury Caucasian dishes. A particular wild variety which does not grow outside the eastern Mediterranean region is much prized.

MINT (*myata*)

A herb ubiquitous in Caucasian and Central Asian cooking, added to tea, salads, many hot savoury dishes and fruit compotes, it marries particularly well with lamb and cucumber, both favoured ingredients.

NUTMEG (*muscatny oreckh*)

A native of the Moluccas in the East Indies, this hard seed of the tree *Myristica fragrans* came north to Russia and Eastern Europe via the Silk Road and then the Baltic ports.

PAPRIKA (*krasny perets*)

A powder ground from the ripened seed pod of the red sweet pepper. The most prized – and sweetest – variety is that known as Hungarian paprika. It is used occasionally in Russian and Ukrainian cooking.

PARSLEY (*petruska kudryavaya*)

Only the flat-leaved variety is used. It has a slightly more marked flavour than the curly strain more commonly found in the West.

SAVORY (*chabyor*)

An atypical member of the mint family, having a sweetly piquant flavour much appreciated in the Georgian kitchen, where it is used in meat stews and marinades.

TARRAGON (*polyn estragon*)

A variety of European wormwood grown for its delicately pungent leaves. It is particularly evident in French and in Georgian cookery; in the latter it complements fish and lamb dishes, as well as vegetables and salads.

SUGGESTED MENUS

A REGIONAL MEDLEY DINNER
Mushroom caviar *(Gribnoy ikra)*
with sour-cream rye rolls
(balabusky)
•
Veal and liver pâté with gherkins and radishes
(Pashtet iz tielyatiny)
(s ogurtsami i ryedisom)
•
Stuffed cabbage rolls
(Golubsty)
•
Sweet apple bread pudding with lemon sauce
(Sladky pudding z yaablokami i limonnoy podlivkoy)

A TRADITIONAL ZAKUSKA DRINKS PARTY
Flavoured vodkas and/or vodka cocktails
•
Uzbekistan sweet walnut brittle
(Sladkoye pyechenye iz gryetskikh orekhov po-Uzbeksky)
•
Miniature salmon and cabbage morsels
(Piroshki z Iososemi Kapustoy)
•
Marinated mushrooms
(Marinovannye Griby)
•
Steak tartare
(Myaso po-Tatarsky)
•
Kazakhstan lamb potato cakes
(Kartophelnye piroshki z baraninoy po-Kazakhsky)
•
Minsk-style eggs
(Jajka Minsky)
•
Deep fried herb and egg envelopes
(Gutap)

A PICNIC EAST OF THE CAUCASUS
Yoghurt soup with apricots and walnuts
(Sup iz yogurta z abricosami i gryetskimi orekhami)
•
Poor man's caviar with toasted pitta bread
(Baklazahannya Ikra)
•
Cold pheasant Georgian-style
(Phazan po-Gruzinsky)
•
Karabakh salad
(Salat po-Karabakhsky)
•
Dried fruit and nut tart
(Tort iz sushyonykh fruktor orekhov)

A HEARTY WINTER LUNCH
Moldovan potato-cheese soup
(Moldavsky sup iz syra i Kartophelya)
•
Siberian ravioli
(Pelmeni)
•
Whipped eggs and sugar
(Gogol-Mogol)
•
Sweet caraway cookies
(Cepumi)

A COLD SUMMER LUNCH PARTY
Raspberry soup
(Malinovyi sup)
•
Lithuanian cottage cheese bacon bread
(Litorsky tworozhny khleb z beconom)
•
Chicken and potato salad
(Salat Olivier)
•
Transcaucasian cabbage and mint salad
(Transcavkazsky salat iz kapusty z myatoy)
•
Uzbekistan sweet walnut brittle
•
Pickled watermelon rind
(Marinovannya arbuznaya korka)
•
Tea ice-cream with rum sauce
(Chainoye morozhennoye z romovoy podlivkoy)

A REGIONAL FISH DINNER
Clear fish consommé with quenelles
(Ukha z Katushkami)
•
Onion-and-mustard herrings
(Sipoli Mércé)
•
Sevan lake trout Yerevan-style
(Sevanskaya fovel po-Yerevansky)
•
Spinach and walnut purée
(Pkhala)
•
Oranges with spiced rum
(Apyelsing v romye z pryanostyami)

~

The Cooking of Court & Capital

Moscow and St Petersburg

———

Greater Russia, even in the heyday of
Communist principle, has always been a land of
haves and have-nots. Nowhere is this more true than
in the two chief cities of the Russian Republic
itself, where the winters are harsh and
scarcity a fact of life.

*The opulent main staircase of the Hermitage Museum in St Petersburg,
one of the world's largest repositories of art, culture and history.*

In the days of empire, good eating was the prerogative of the aristocracy and the merchant classes; the peasants continued as they had for centuries at subsistence level. The triumph of the socialist state simply meant that that level was extended upwards, to give the greater number the opportunity to live, literally, on the breadline. The political elite, the *politburo* chiefs and state *apparatchiks*, continued to enjoy privileges denied the masses. Like the tsars and nobility of old, they had specialist suppliers and sources denied the common man. While the tsar had commanded his own fishing and hunting grounds, and was liberally gifted by foreign ambassadors with wines, cheeses and other delicacies, they had access to hard-currency supermarkets and the expensive state-run *Beryoskas*, selling imported luxuries like instant coffee, alcoholic drinks and sugar, as well as homegrown smoked sturgeon, caviar and champagne (*shampanskoye*).

Even the geographical locales did not change. Moscow and Leningrad (now reverted to its pre-revolutionary name of St Petersburg) continued as the dominant centres of the politics, learning, arts and culture – in its widest sense – of the Russian Republic, and thus of the Union of Socialist States. Those few visitors who ventured behind the Iron Curtain almost inevitably went to these two historic capitals; but the uninspired, and often downright unpalatable, fare they sampled there had become a travesty of the great days of 19th- and early 20th-century *haute cuisine*.

That overused phrase is no misnomer in this case. Many dishes which later became internationally known were culinarily translated from the Russian colloquial by gifted French chefs. The great Anton Carême, who cooked for Alexander (*Alexi*) I, is probably the most famous, but many others followed in his wake, working not only for the royal family but also for the lesser nobility. Ethnic influences from the Russian heartland, from rich estates in the Ukraine and Belorussia, and from the lands of the south, were refined by these culinary artists into recipes still exotic but now appealing to cultivated tastes. Dishes like *bef Stroganov*, *charlotte Russe*, *steak Tartare* and *rum baba* spread from Russian to Parisian society, and on to the *nouveau riche* tables of Delmonicos in New York.

A COSMOPOLITAN CUISINE

It is not only to the French, however, that the classics of the high table owe thanks. Earlier, trade with Byzantium and the exploitation and final annexation of Georgia, Armenia and the Central Asian States had resulted in a range of wines, a tradition of sweet cakes and pastries, and an appreciation of fresh fruit and nuts. In the early 18th century, Peter the Great employed Dutch, German and Swedish chefs. An initially bemused, then enthusiastic, court was introduced to sausages, hard cheese, fruit sauces and compotes.

Perhaps it was the Swedes more than anyone, however, who influenced the style of entertaining, by tempting the hearty Russian appetite with an initial medley of titbits – smoked fish, caviar, cold ham, preserved vegetables and savoury pastries. An adaptation of their own beloved *smörgåsbord*, it was christened *zakuski* (small bites) in Russian. By the last years of the 19th century, it had evolved into an intricate marriage of the culinary and visual arts so lavish that foreigners understandably mistook it for the whole meal. The growing middle class in pre-Revolutionary Russia took the custom to their hearts and tables. Even in today's straitened circumstances, nowhere is the generosity and imagination of the native character made more apparent than in this traditional first act of a meal.

TRAVELLER'S TALES

Today, the changes shaking up the Russian Republic present the visitor to Moscow and St Petersburg with an uncomfortable paradox and a new variation on the theme of haves and have-nots. While tourists can eat well – and, more and more, exceptionally well – at the new co-operative restaurants, with a strict policy of hard currency only, which have sprung up all over both cities, on the streets the locals jostle to sell their services and possessions for food. If lucky they will join the snaking queues at low-quality rouble cafés and shops, unless they have obtained dollars from a Western source.

It is difficult not to feel guilty at being able to buy a better lifestyle than the people who live there. At the same time it is frustrating for the true traveller, who wants to experience a country without the divisive trappings that mark him or her as alien. Yet attempting to patronize restaurants where the Russians go can mean indifferent-to-awful food, long queues, and sometimes simply no success. A room of empty tables will be unaccountably declared full – and off you are sent to a hard currency establishment made for the likes of you.

It is to be hoped that the quality of the new restaurants will remain, while the restrictions on clientele and supply will eventually be eliminated. This, of course, would be the happy result of economic stability and reform for the entire country. At present, however, tourism is one of the few bright prospects for the historic capitals of Old Russia. Since the Iron Curtain has been torn asunder, the Western world has been looking – and venturing – in with as much curiosity as Russia's citizens have been looking out.

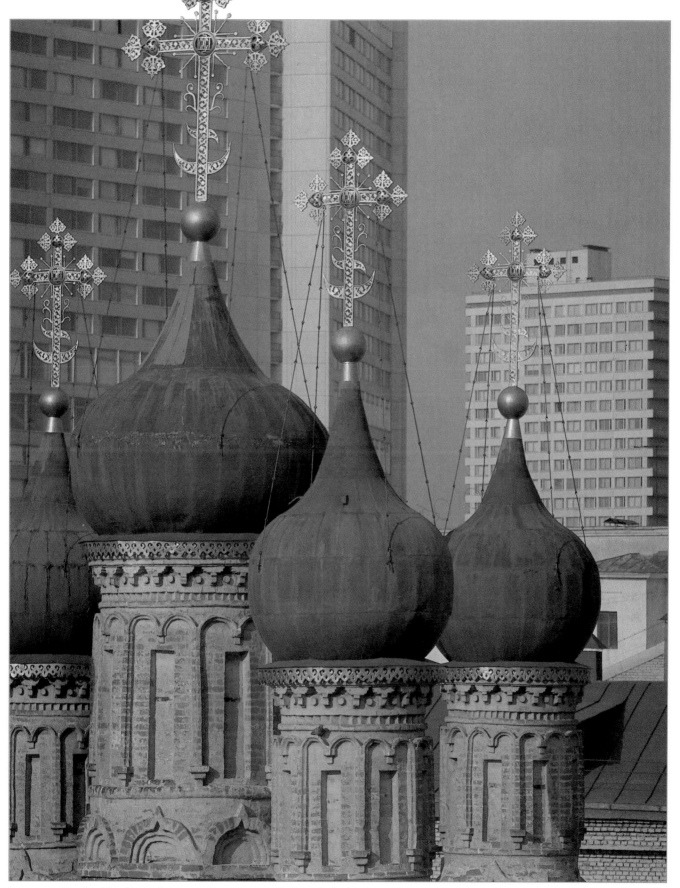

On Arbat Street, the towers of a Russian Orthodox cathedral and modern skyscrapers epitomize Moscow old and new.

Clear Fish Consommé with Quenelles

CLEAR FISH CONSOMMÉ WITH QUENELLES

UKHA Z KATUSHKI

◆ ◆ ◆

Usually made with sturgeon in Russia, this light consommé can also be served with fish *pelmeni* (Siberian ravioli) instead of *katushki*, giving a Siberian twist.

SERVES 6–8

- ◆ *2.25 l/4 pts water*
- ◆ *225 ml/8 fl oz dry white wine*
- ◆ *1.75 kg/4 lb fish bones and trimmings from white fish*
- ◆ *2 large onions, sliced*
- ◆ *2 large carrots, thickly sliced*
- ◆ *6 parsley sprigs*

- ◆ *1 bay leaf*
- ◆ *2 whole cloves*
- ◆ *1 tsp black peppercorns*
- ◆ *30 ml/2 tbsp fresh lemon juice*
- ◆ *1 tbsp finely chopped fresh dill*

For the *katushki*

- ◆ *675 g/1¹/₂ lb white fish (haddock, pike, whiting fillets)*
- ◆ *3 x 2 cm/³/₄ in thick Greek, sour dough or country-style white bread, crusts removed and soaked in a little water*

- ◆ *1 egg*
- ◆ *¹/₂ tsp fresh dill, finely chopped*
- ◆ *salt and freshly ground black pepper*
- ◆ *flour*

To make a *court bouillon*, place the water in a large saucepan and set over a high heat. Add the wine, fish trimmings, onions, carrots, parsley, bay leaf, cloves and peppercorns. Bring to the boil and simmer strongly until reduced by half – about 1 hour or a little more. Remove the carrots.

Pour the *court bouillon* into a bowl. Rinse the saucepan and place a sieve over it. Line with damp muslin and pour the *bouillon* into it. When the liquid has drained through, press the solids with a spoon to extract as much juice as possible, then twist the muslin over the bowl to get the last drops. Discard the fish trimmings and vegetables. (The *bouillon* may be made in advance and chilled or frozen until needed.)

Now make the *katushki*. Remove any small bones from the fish and squeeze out the bread as much as possible. Process the bread and fish to a rough paste in a food processor or blender then place in a bowl with the egg, seasoning to taste, and the dill. Knead with the hands until you have a firm mixture (if the mixture is not thick enough, add a little flour until it takes firm shape). Take out small handfuls of the mixture and form into olive shapes about 2 cm/³/₄ in in diameter. Chill the quenelles for about 1 hour. (They may be kept in the refrigerator overnight.)

When ready to serve the soup, return the *court bouillon* to a saucepan and bring to the boil. Reduce the heat to low, thinly slice the reserved carrots, and return to the saucepan. Gently drop in the *katushki*. Simmer the *katushki* in the broth until they are cooked, abut 10 minutes, then add the lemon juice. Spoon into individual bowls and garnish with dill.

SORREL SOUP WITH KIDNEYS AND GHERKINS

RASSOLNIK

◆ ◆ ◆

A soup which crept from lowly origins to the highest tables in the land. This is a St Petersburg favourite, served chilled as often as hot.

SERVES 8

- ◆ *75 g/3 oz butter*
- ◆ *50 ml/2 fl oz vegetable or sunflower oil*
- ◆ *1 medium onion, finely chopped*
- ◆ *1 celery stick, finely chopped*
- ◆ *1 medium carrot, finely chopped*
- ◆ *1 large potato, peeled and diced*
- ◆ *450 g/1 lb lamb's kidneys, trimmed and cut into 1 cm/¹/₂ in pieces*
- ◆ *50 g/2 oz plain flour*
- ◆ *6 parsley sprigs, chopped*

- ◆ *900 g/2 lb fresh sorrel leaves or 450 g/1 lb each sorrel and young spinach leaves, stripped from their stems and finely chopped*
- ◆ *salt and freshly ground black pepper*
- ◆ *1.5 l/2 ¹/₂ pt beef stock*
- ◆ *1 bay leaf*
- ◆ *2 sour kosher gherkins, finely chopped, with*
- ◆ *75 ml/3 fl oz pickling juices*
- ◆ *1 egg yolk*
- ◆ *sour cream*

Melt 50 g/2 oz butter and 30 ml/2 tbsp oil in a large saucepan and gently sauté the onion, celery and carrot until they are softened and lightly coloured, about 10 minutes. Add the chopped potato and continue cooking, stirring for a further 5 minutes. Transfer the vegetables to a bowl and set aside.

Heat the remaining butter and oil in the pan. Dip the kidney pieces into the flour and gently fry them until they are slightly browned, about 3 minutes. Remove with a slotted spoon and set aside. Stir the parsley and sorrel (or sorrel and spinach) into the pan and add the cooked vegetables. Toss everything gently until the leaves are wilted. Season to taste with salt and pepper and add the beef stock and bay leaf. Bring to the boil, then cover, lower the heat and simmer for about 25 minutes.

Remove the bay leaf and mash the vegetables to thicken the soup. Stir in the gherkins and their juice, together with the cooked kidneys. Simmer for a further 5 minutes.

Remove a cupful of the soup and beat with the egg yolk in a small bowl. Stir the egg mixture back into the soup and heat it briefly. Do not boil or the egg will curdle.

If serving hot, transfer the soup to a large tureen and pass the sour cream separately. If serving cold, cool to room temperature, then chill for 2-3 hours before dividing between individual bowls, each topped with a spoonful of sour cream.

ASPARAGUS VEAL BROTH

BAGRATION

◆ ◆ ◆

This elegant consommé was named for Prince Bagration, the Georgian general felled by Napoleon's troops at the Battle of Borodino, outside Moscow, in 1812. Though the battle ended in a draw, it marked an important moment in Russian nationalism, culminating in the French emperor's ignominious retreat from the capital.

SERVES 6

- ◆ 50 ml/2 fl oz sunflower oil
- ◆ 1.5 kg/3 lb veal trimmings and bones
- ◆ 2 large onions, finely chopped
- ◆ 2 large carrots, peeled and chopped
- ◆ 2 x 400 ml/14 fl oz cans of chicken consommé
- ◆ 2 bay leaves
- ◆ ½ tsp crumbled fresh thyme
- ◆ 3 egg whites
- ◆ salt and freshly ground white pepper
- ◆ 450 g/1 lb baby asparagus tips
- ◆ sour cream
- ◆ fresh dill sprigs

Heat the oil in a large saucepan. Add the veal trimmings and bones and toss them in the oil over medium heat until browned all over, about 15-20 minutes.

Add the chopped vegetables and continue to cook until they are lightly coloured and softened. Add the chicken consommé, bay leaves and thyme, adding water, if necessary, to cover the meat, bones and vegetables. Bring to the boil and continue to cook vigorously for 15 minutes, skimming off the scum that rises to the surface. Then reduce the heat, cover, and simmer for 2 hours.

Allow the stock to cool slightly then strain it into a bowl, pressing hard on the meat and vegetables to extract as much juice a possible. Cover, cool and chill for at least 12 hours or overnight.

Pour half the stock into containers and freeze for future use. Of the remainder, pour 300 ml/½ pt into a large bowl and the rest into a saucepan.

Beat the egg whites into the stock in the bowl. Bring the stock in the saucepan to the boil then in a stream, pour into the egg-white stock, beating all the while. Pour the combined stock into the saucepan and bring to a simmer over moderate heat, whisking constantly. When just simmering, reduce the heat to low, stop stirring, and let the stock simmer uncovered for 25 minutes.

Line a sieve with several layers of muslin or absorbent kitchen paper and place over a clean saucepan. Slowly ladle the stock and congealed egg whites into the sieve, trying to disturb the whites as little as possible. The resultant consommé should be clear and delicate, leaving the impurities adhering to the whites in the sieve.

Place the strained stock over high heat. Season to taste with salt and white pepper and bring to the boil. Add the asparagus tips and cook for about 4 minutes. Divide the asparagus between the bowls and ladle the consommé over it. Garnish each serving with a dollop of sour cream and a fresh dill sprig.

MUSHROOM CAVIAR

GRIBNOY IKRA

◆ ◆ ◆

Eastern Europeans, particularly Russians and Poles, are mushroom fanatics. Dawn expeditions into the wooded countryside in search of fungi are a common sight in autumn.

SERVES 8–10

- ◆ *350 g/12 oz fresh mushrooms (the more varieties, the better – field, shiitake, oyster, girolle, etc), finely chopped*
- ◆ *1 medium onion, finely chopped*
- ◆ *100 g/4 oz butter*
- ◆ *15 ml/1 tbsp dry sherry*
- ◆ *75 g/3 oz curd cheese*
- ◆ *75 g/3 oz full-fat cream cheese*
- ◆ *50 g/2 oz fresh parsley finely chopped*
- ◆ *25 g/ 1 oz fresh tarragon finely chopped*
- ◆ *25 g/1 oz fresh marjoram, finely chopped*

In a large frying pan, sauté the mushrooms and onion in the butter over medium heat, stirring often. When the mushrooms are browned and softened, add the sherry. Remove from the heat.

In a bowl, beat together the two cheeses and herbs. Stir in the mushrooms, onion and their juices. Beat the mixture with a wooden spoon until it is well combined. Spoon the pâté into a small crock, smooth, swirl the top and cover. Chill overnight or up to three days before serving with small rye rounds.

VEAL AND LIVER PÂTÉ

PASHTET IZ TIELYATINY

◆ ◆ ◆

Pashtet **can be made with veal and liver, pork and liver, or just liver; it can be served plain, set in aspic or baked in pastry. This is a fairly simple recipe enlivened with dried mushrooms, a favourite Ukrainian ingredient.**

SERVES 8

- ◆ *225 g/8 oz calves' liver, chopped*
- ◆ *225 ml/8 fl oz milk*
- ◆ *50 g/2 oz butter*
- ◆ *225 g/8 oz streaky bacon, sliced*
- ◆ *1 small onion, chopped*
- ◆ *1 stick celery, chopped*
- ◆ *1 small carrot, chopped*
- ◆ *1 bay leaf*
- ◆ *4 peppercorns*
- ◆ *225 g/8 oz lean veal, chopped*
- ◆ *225 ml/8 fl oz chicken consommé or stock*
- ◆ *75 g/3 oz dried boletus or porcini mushrooms*
- ◆ *2 slices stale white bread, crusts removed*
- ◆ *2 small eggs*
- ◆ *pinch of allspice*
- ◆ *salt and freshly ground black pepper*

In a bowl, soak the calves' liver in the milk for 1 hour. Drain thoroughly and discard the milk.

In a frying pan with a lid, melt the butter over medium heat and coarsely chop and fry 175 g/6 oz of the bacon for 3–4 minutes. Add the onion, celery, carrot, bay leaf, peppercorns and veal; toss to coat in the bacon fat and butter for a few minutes. Then pour over the chicken stock and add the dried mushrooms. Cover and simmer gently for 1 hour. Add the liver and cook for a further 30 minutes.

Remove from the heat. Strain the stock into a bowl and soak the bread in it for 5 minutes. Squeeze out as much moisture from the bread as possible and process in batches with the meat and vegetables in a blender or a processor fitted with a metal blade. As the mixture is ground up, transfer to a large bowl. With the hands, work in the eggs, allspice and salt and more pepper to taste.

Preheat the oven to 180°C/350°F/Gas Mark 4. Line a 9x5x3 in loaf tin with the remaining bacon. Pack in the meat mixture, smooth the top, and cover the tin with foil. Bake for 45–60 minutes, until the pâté is browned and a wooden cocktail stick inserted in it comes away clean. Cool, remove from the tin, then chill. Serve in thick slices with black bread and butter and pickled gherkins.

Buckwheat Crêpes with Caviar

BUCKWHEAT CREPES WITH CAVIAR

BLINI Z IKRA

◆ ◆ ◆

Leaving the batter for the *blinis* to stand overnight allows it to acquire its distinctive sour flavour. *Blinis* freeze well, and are delicious paired with smoked salmon or smoked meats such as ham and turkey and with cottage cheese accompanied by dried or fresh soft fruits.

SERVES 8–10

- ◆ *90 ml/3 fl oz lukewarm water*
- ◆ *2¹/₂ tsp (8 g/¹/₄ oz packet) active dry yeast*
- ◆ *2 tbsp sugar*
- ◆ *450 ml/16 fl oz milk*
- ◆ *225 g/8 oz unsalted butter, melted*
- ◆ *100 g/4 oz buckwheat flour*
- ◆ *100 g/4 oz plain flour*
- ◆ *1 tsp salt*
- ◆ *2 large eggs, separated, at room temperature*
- ◆ *175 ml/6 fl oz sour cream*
- ◆ *225 g/8 oz black caviar or lumpfish roe*
- ◆ *225 g/8 oz golden or red salmon roe*

Pour the lukewarm water into a small bowl. Sprinkle the yeast and ¹/₂ tbsp sugar over it and leave for 3 minutes. Stir to dissolve completely, then set in a warm spot for another five minutes, until it is foamy and doubled in volume.

Heat 225 ml/8 fl oz milk to lukewarm and stir into the yeast mixture together with the remaining sugar and 25 g/1 oz butter. Beat in the buckwheat flour for about 1¹/₂ minutes, then cover tightly with cling film and chill it overnight.

Next day, let the batter come to room temperature. Heat 225 ml/8 fl oz milk to lukewarm and stir into the batter together with the plain flour, salt, egg yolks and sour cream. Beat the mixture for about 1 minute, then cover and leave to rise for 1 hour or until foamy and double in size. In a metal bowl, beat the egg whites to stiff peaks. Fold them gently into the batter.

Place a griddle or a shallow frying pan over medium heat and, when it is hot, brush lightly with butter. Drop about 30 ml/2 tbsp batter on to the griddle so that it spreads into a 7.5–10 cm/3–4 in circle. Repeat twice and fry the blinis for 2 minutes, or until the undersides are golden. Brush the tops lightly with melted butter and turn them over to cook for 1 more minute. Repeat until all the batter is used up, meanwhile keeping the blinis warm, covered with foil, in the oven set at 120°C/250°F/Gas Mark ¹/₂. (The blinis may be made up to 2 days before and kept covered and chilled. Reheat in a 180°C/350°F/Gas Mark 4 oven for 15 minutes.)

Serve the warm blinis wrapped in a napkin on a heated platter, accompanied by pots of the caviar and roe in ice and an attractive arrangement of sour cream, finely chopped hard-boiled egg, sliced lemon and snipped dill.

EGGS À LA RUSSE

YAITSA PO-RUSSKI

◆ ◆ ◆

While the origins of this dish lie within the borders of the Austro-Hungarian rather than the Russian Empire – it was a favourite of turn-of-the-century Viennese chefs – the marriage of ingredients justifies the name they gave it.

SERVES 6

◆ 6 hard-boiled eggs, halved
◆ 30 ml/2 tbsp mayonnaise
◆ $\frac{1}{2}$ tsp dry mustard powder
◆ 15 ml/1 tbsp Dijon mustard
◆ 3 tbsp finely chopped sour-sweet gherkins
◆ 2 tsp finely chopped spring onion
◆ salt and freshly ground black pepper

To garnish
◆ capers ◆ paprika

Remove the yolks from the halved eggs, reserving the whites, and place them in a small bowl. Mash them thoroughly, then blend the mayonnaise, the two mustards, the chopped gherkins, spring onion and seasoning to taste. Spoon the mixture into the egg-white halves and garnish decoratively with the capers and paprika.

MINIATURE SALMON-CABBAGE MORSELS

PIROSHKI Z LOSOSEM I KAPUSTOY

◆ ◆ ◆

These *piroshki* are wrapped in yeast dough, a Ukrainian influence. Their contents and small size make them just the ticket for stylish drinks parties. Raise a glass of Abrau-Durso – Russian champagne – and down one of these little treats!

MAKES ABOUT 20

- ◆ 2–3 dried boletus or other wild mushrooms
- ◆ 450 g/1 lb cabbage, cored and trimmed of old leaves
- ◆ 45 g/1¹/₂ oz unsalted butter
- ◆ salt and freshly ground black pepper
- ◆ 100 g/4 oz salmon fillet
- ◆ 30 ml/2 tbsp sour cream
- ◆ 1 tbsp caraway seeds
- ◆ 1 tbsp dill seeds
- ◆ 1 egg

For the dough

- ◆ 50 ml/2 fl oz lukewarm water
- ◆ 1 tbsp caster sugar
- ◆ 2¹/₂ tsp (8 g/¹/₄ oz packet) active dry yeast
- ◆ 400 g/14 oz plain flour
- ◆ 1¹/₂ tsp salt
- ◆ 175 ml/6 fl oz warm milk
- ◆ 90 g/3¹/₂ oz unsalted butter, melted
- ◆ 2 large eggs
- ◆ oil

Make the dough first. Place the water in a small bowl and sprinkle 1 tsp sugar and the yeast over it. Leave to stand for 15 minutes or until foamy. In a larger bowl, combine three-quarters of the flour with the salt. Make a well in the centre and pour in the yeast mixture, the milk, the melted butter, the eggs and the rest of the sugar. Using your hands, turn the dry ingredients into the wet and combine thoroughly until you have a soft dough. Remove to a floured board and knead, adding more flour if necessary, to keep it pliable and not sticky. Continue kneading until the dough begins to blister.

Form the dough into a ball with your hands and place it in an oiled bowl, turning to cover with oil. Cover with cling film and let the dough rise in a warm place until it has doubled. Knock it down, cover and chill overnight.

To make the filling, soak the mushrooms in hot water for 30 minutes. Drain and chop them finely. Shred the cabbage in a food processor, then chop into shorter lengths. Place in a large saucepan of boiling water and boil for 3 minutes. Drain, refresh under cold water and drain again, squeezing out the excess water.

In a large frying pan, sauté the cabbage in the butter for about 15 minutes. Season to taste and stir in the salmon and the mushrooms, tossing just enough to combine. Stir in the sour cream, then the caraway and dill seeds. Take off the heat, cool, then chill for 30 minutes.

Divide the ball of dough in half. Return one half to the fridge and roll out the other into a thin rectangle. Cut out 9 cm/3¹/₂ in rounds with a biscuit cutter or lid. Reserve the scraps.

Preheat the oven to 200°C/400°F/Gas Mark 6. Make an egg wash by beating the egg with a pinch of salt. Place a heaped teaspoon of the filling on each round, brush the edges with some of the wash, and fold over to make a crescent, pinching the edges together. Use the scraps to make further *piroshki*. Place them on a lightly greased baking sheet, cover with a towel, and allow to rise for 15–20 minutes. Brush the tops with the wash and bake in the oven for 20–25 minutes or until lightly golden.

Roll out the remaining dough and bake in a similar fashion. (The *piroshki* can be baked ahead and frozen. Defrost and reheat at 180C/350°F/Gas Mark 4 for 10–15 minutes.)

A distinguished feature of the Mikhailovsk Bridge in St Petersburg are its cast-iron fences.

CHICKEN LIVERS IN MADEIRA SAUCE

PYECHYEN KUR V MADERE

◆ ◆ ◆

Served on its own, this recipe is a classic *zakuska*. but it is so delicious – and so rich – that it would make an elegant and inexpensive main course. Spoon it over rice or, more authentically, use to fill dinner-sized vol-au-vents.

SERVES 4–6

- ◆ *675 g/1¹/₂ lb chicken livers .*
- ◆ *milk*
- ◆ *50 g/2 oz butter*
- ◆ *1 onion, sliced*
- ◆ *salt and freshly ground black pepper*
- ◆ *100 g/4 oz flour*
- ◆ *175 ml/6 fl oz chicken stock*
- ◆ *100 ml/4 fl oz Madeira*
- ◆ *90 ml/3¹/₂ fl oz sour cream*
- ◆ *fresh parsley, finely chopped*

Immerse the chicken livers in milk to just cover and soak for 2 hours. Drain thoroughly and discard the milk.

Melt the butter over medium heat and sauté the onion until softened. Dip the chicken livers in seasoned flour and add to the onions. Fry gently until just coloured, about 5 minutes. Stir in the stock and the Madeira, cover, and simmer for about 10 minutes, or until the livers are tender. Season the sauce to taste.

Transfer the livers to a bowl; boil the sauce until it is well reduced. Turn down the heat and whisk in the sour cream, a little at a time. Return the livers to the pan, spoon the sauce over and heat through gently. Serve immediately, sprinkled with fresh parsley.

CHICKEN OR VEAL AND PORK CUTLETS

KOTLETY POJARSKI

◆ ◆ ◆

These patties are encountered all over Russia in varying degrees of digestibility – from execrable to excellent. The latter are frequently served with the sauce given below.

SERVES 6

- ◆ *675 g/1¹/₂ lb minced chicken or mixture of 350 g/12 oz each veal and pork,well-chilled*
- ◆ *175 g/6 oz fine fresh breadcrumbs*
- ◆ *75 g/3 oz unsalted butter, softened*
- ◆ *100 ml/4 fl oz double cream*
- ◆ *large pinch of nutmeg*
- ◆ *salt and freshly ground black pepper*
- ◆ *2 large eggs, beaten*
- ◆ *30 ml/2 tbsp vegetable oil*

For the sauce

- ◆ *50 g/2 oz unsalted butter*
- ◆ *1 small onion, chopped*
- ◆ *225 ml/8 fl oz dry white wine*
- ◆ *225 ml/8 fl oz chicken or beef stock*
- ◆ *2 tsp flour*
- ◆ *15 ml/1 tbsp Dijon-style mustard*
- ◆ *30 ml/2 tbsp fresh lemon juice or sour cream*

In a blender or a food processor, combine the minced meat with 50 g/2 oz breadcrumbs, 50 g/2 oz butter, the cream, nutmeg and salt and pepper to taste. Process until the mixture reaches the consistency of paste. Remove, form into 6 cutlet-shaped patties, and place on greaseproof paper. Chill for at least 2 hours.

Meanwhile, start the sauce. In a stainless steel or enamel saucepan, melt 45 g/1¹/₂ oz butter and gently sauté the onion until it is softened. Stir in the white wine and the stock and bring to the boil. Reduce the heat and simmer, uncovered, for about 10 minutes, then set aside.

Using your fingers, knead the flour into the remaining butter to make a *beurre manié*. Increase the heat of the stock and drop in the *beurre manié* bit by bit, stirring all the time. When the sauce is thickened, remove from the heat.

Take the cutlets from the refrigerator. Place the beaten eggs in a shallow bowl and the remaining breadcrumbs on a plate. Dip each of the cutlets into the beaten egg, shaking off the excess, and then press into the breadcrumbs, coating each side well. Chill for another hour.

Heat the remaining butter and the oil in a large saucepan and fry the cutlets, 3 at a time, over medium-high heat for 4–5 minutes each side, or until golden-brown and cooked through. Remove and keep warm.

Finish the sauce by reheating it gently, stirring. Stir in the mustard and lemon juice or sour cream.

CHICKEN AND POTATO SALAD

SALAT OLIVIER

◆ ◆ ◆

A near relative of the 'Russian salad' so dear to the hearts of caterers and delicatessen owners, this real Russian salad is a traditional favourite, again refined and Frenchified by an imported chef. It would make a delicious main course for a summer luncheon or picnic.

SERVES 6

- 675 g/1^1/$_2$ lb cooked, boned and skinned chicken
- 5 hard-boiled eggs
- 225 g/8 oz new or small red potatoes, boiled in their skins and thinly sliced
- 100 g/4 oz cooked fresh or frozen peas, drained
- 2 large sour gherkins, finely chopped
- 175 ml/6 fl oz mayonnaise
- 100 ml/4 fl oz sour cream
- 10 ml/2 tsp Worcestershire sauce
- salt and freshly ground black pepper
- 100 g/4 oz black olives, halved
- 15 ml/1 tbsp chopped fresh dill
- 2 tbsp capers

Slice the chicken into 1 cm/^{1}/$_2$ in wide strips. Finely chop two of the eggs. Place the chicken and chopped eggs in a large bowl, together with the potatoes, peas and gherkins. In a smaller bowl, beat together the mayonnaise and the sour cream. Fold the Worcestershire sauce and half the dressing into the chicken mixture, seasoning to taste.

To serve in the Russian manner, mound the chicken salad in the centre of a large serving dish. Slice the remaining eggs and arrange the slices around the salad. Top each slice with a halved olive. Spoon the remaining dressing over the salad and scatter the chopped dill and capers over the top. Chill for 30 minutes before serving.

BEEF STROGANOFF

BEF STROGANOV

◆ ◆ ◆

The Stroganovs became one of the wealthiest members of the merchant aristocracy through their exploitation of Siberia's fur resources. The French chef of a late 19th-century Count Stroganov created this now internationally popular dish. It should *not* be served over rice – a heresy introduced by the West – but a tuft of straw potatoes on top is classically acceptable.

SERVES 6–8

- *1 tbsp dry mustard powder*
- *1 tbsp sugar*
- *90 ml/6 tbsp sunflower oil*
- *3 large onions, sliced*
- *450 g/1 lb fresh button or field mushrooms, sliced*
- *1.25 kg/2¹/₂ lb fresh beef fillet, cut into 1 cm/¹/₂ in wide strips*
- *salt and freshly ground black pepper*
- *600 ml/1 pt sour cream*
- *6 fresh parsley sprigs, stems removed, chopped*
- *deep-fried straw potatoes (optional)*

Combine the mustard and sugar in a bowl with water to make a paste. Let the flavours mingle while completing the recipe.

Heat half the sunflower oil in a large, heavy-bottomed shallow casserole. When just crackling, add the sliced onions, reduce the heat to low, and stir. Gently soften the onions, covered, for about 25 minutes, stirring occasionally. During the last 10 minutes, uncover and add the mushrooms. Remove from the heat, drain the mixture, and set aside in a bowl.

Heat the remaining oil in the casserole. Drop in half the meat, stirring with a wooden spoon and turning the strips over to brown evenly. Transfer with a slotted spoon to the bowl with the vegetables; sauté the remaining meat. When all is browned, return the meat and vegetables to the casserole, together with the mustard mixture. Season to taste and add the sour cream, a little at a time, stirring continuously. Cover the casserole, heat through gently for about 5 minutes, and serve. Top each serving with a light scattering of parsley, and the straw potatoes, if desired.

SADDLE OF VENISON

SEDLO OLENYA

◆ ◆ ◆

The aristocrat of game dishes, today venison is rarely seen on even the most expensive restaurant menus in the major cities. Only in the wooded countryside, particularly in the belt around St Petersburg, can families enjoy this prize of the hunter's bag.

SERVES 6–8

- ◆ *2.25 kg/5 lb saddle of young venison*
- ◆ *salt and freshly ground black pepper*
- ◆ *8 slices streaky bacon*
- ◆ *450 ml/³/₄ pt beef stock*
- ◆ *175 ml/6 fl oz sour cream*
- ◆ *1 tsp grated horseradish*

For the marinade

- ◆ *225 ml/8 fl oz dry white wine*
- ◆ *100 ml/4 fl oz olive oil*
- ◆ *1 large onion, thinly sliced*
- ◆ *2 cloves garlic, crushed*
- ◆ *20 black peppercorns*
- ◆ *2 tsp dried thyme*

Make the marinade first. Combine all the marinade ingredients in a large, shallow dish and blend well. Add the venison to the dish, turn to coat, and set aside to marinate at room temperature for 24 hours. Baste occasionally.

Heat the oven to 230C/450°F/Gas Mark 8. Remove the venison from the marinade and pat dry with absorbent kitchen paper. Pour the marinade through a strainer and set it aside.

Using your fingertips, rub the venison all over with salt and pepper. Put it on a rack in a large, deep roasting tin and arrange the bacon over the top. Pour the reserved marinade and stock into the roasting tin and place in the preheated oven. Roast for 30 minutes.

Reduce the temperature to 180°C/350°F/Gas Mark 4. Cook the venison, basting every 15 minutes, for a further 1¹/₄–1¹/₂ hours until it is tender.

Remove the venison from the oven and transfer to a carving board; discard the bacon. Pour the pan liquid into a small saucepan and bring to the boil over high heat. Reduce to low and stir in the cream and horseradish. Simmer for a couple of minutes until the sauce is warm. Transfer to a warmed sauceboat.

Carve the venison into thick slices and arrange on a platter. Serve immediately with the sauce.

FRUIT PURÉE DESSERT

KISEL

◆ ◆ ◆

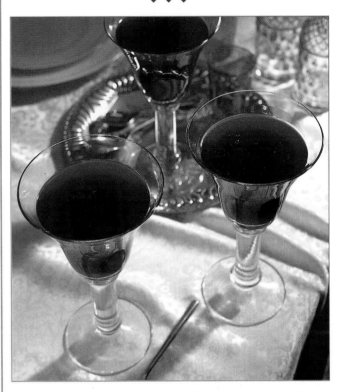

***Kisel* is a traditional summer dessert, changing its character as the different fruits come into season. It can also be thinned to become a sweet drink, a summer treat in the days before coke and fizzy drinks became the norm, even in Russia.**

SERVES 4–6

- ◆ *450 g/1 lb raspberries, strawberries, blueberries, cherries, peeled apricots or peaches*
- ◆ *600 ml/1 pt water*
- ◆ *100 g/4 oz sugar*
- ◆ *2–2¹/₂ tbsp arrowroot*
- ◆ *150 ml/¹/₄ pt white or red wine (optional)*

Place the washed and cleaned fruit into a saucepan with the water. Bring to the boil, then simmer for 15–20 minutes. The fruit should be very pulpy. Strain the liquid from the fruit into a bowl. Be careful not to press on the fruit too hard; it will make the juice cloudy.

Discard the solids and return the juice to the saucepan, together with the sugar. Bring to the boil, then lower the heat and simmer. In a small bowl, whisk the arrowroot with 60 ml/4 tbsp of the juice (use 2 tbsp arrowroot if not including the wine; otherwise, add 2¹/₂ tbsp). Stir the thickening into the juice and the wine, if using. Continue to simmer, whisking, for a few minutes. Remove from the heat, cool slightly, pour into individual glasses and chill for at least 4 hours before serving.

CHARLOTTE RUSSE

CHARLOTTKA

◆ ◆ ◆

This famous dessert was the creation of Anton Carême, chef to Tsar Alexander I in the first quarter of the 19th century. The great French cook exploited the Russian love of fruit purées – charlottkas usually have apple or soft fruit fillings or accompanying sauces. This popular version makes use of apricot custard.

SERVES 8–9

- ◆ 15–30 ml/1–2 tbsp apricot jam
- ◆ 16–18 sponge fingers
- ◆ 150 ml/¹/₄ pt whipping or double cream
- ◆ 100 ml/4 fl oz can baby mandarin segments, drained

For the custard filling

- ◆ 450 g/1 lb can apricot halves in syrup, drained and syrup reserved
- ◆ 25 ml/5 tsp gelatine
- ◆ 8 egg yolks
- ◆ 100 g/4 oz sugar
- ◆ 300 ml/¹/₂ pt milk
- ◆ 175 ml/6 fl oz double cream
- ◆ 100 ml/4 fl oz sour cream
- ◆ 90 ml/6 tbsp Cointreau, Grand Marnier or other orange liqueur

Spread the jam thinly around the inside edge of a 20–23 cm/8–9 in, deep springform tin. Measure the biscuits against the sides of the tin and cut off one end so that they will stand up. Line them up side-to-side, around the inside of the tin, pressing them into the jam.

Make the purée and custard filling. Place the drained fruit in a blender or a food processor fitted with the metal blade. Add 100 ml/4 fl oz of the apricot syrup and purée the apricots. Place 45 ml/3 tbsp apricot syrup in a small bowl and sprinkle the gelatine into it. Put the bowl into a pan of hot water and stir the syrup and gelatine until the latter has dissolved.

Beat the egg yolks with the sugar in a bowl placed over a pan of hot water until the mixture is creamy and lemon yellow. Bring the milk to simmering point and slowly stir it into the egg mixture, stirring all the time. Continue to stir over the hot water until the mixture has become a spoon-coating custard. Stir the gelatine into the custard, take off the heat and allow to cool to room temperature.

Whisk the apricot purée into the custard, then cover and chill in the refrigerator until the mixture is satiny and just beginning to set. In a bowl, combine the double cream and sour cream and whip until they reach stiff peak stage. Fold into the apricot mixture, together with the orange liqueur.

Pour the mixture into the biscuit-lined tin. Chill for 4 hours or overnight.

To unmould, run a knife around between the tin and the biscuits. Spring open the tin and slip the charlotte out. Whip the whipping or double cream, fill a piping bag and circle the top of the charlotte with piped rosettes. Place a mandarin segment on top of each rosette. Keep chilled until served.

TEA ICE CREAM WITH RUM SAUCE

CHAINOYE MOROZHENNOYE Z ROMOVOY PODLIVKOY

◆ ◆ ◆

This is an updated version of a dessert once served in the grand salons of Russian nobility. Elegant and light, it comes from the Silk Road through Central Asia and Caucasia

SERVES 8

- ◆ *100 g/4 oz kumquats, trimmed and finely chopped*
- ◆ *100 g/4 oz caster sugar*
- ◆ *30 ml/2 tbsp water*
- ◆ *2 tbsp shelled pistachios*
- ◆ *5 tbsp black tea leaves*
- ◆ *75 ml/3 fl oz boiling water*
- ◆ *5 large egg yolks*
- ◆ *350 ml/12 fl oz double cream*
- ◆ *3 large egg whites*
- ◆ *50 g/2 oz icing sugar*

For the topping

- ◆ *2 tbsp icing sugar*
- ◆ *15 ml/1 tbsp golden rum*
- ◆ *100 ml/4 fl oz cold double cream*

In a small saucepan, combine the kumquats with half the caster sugar and the water. Bring to the boil, stirring, then lower the heat and simmer, stirring frequently, until the kumquats are pulpy. Let the mixture cool and drain off the excess liquid.

Pour boiling water over the pistachios and leave for 1 minute. Drain and rub off the skins.

Place the boiling water in a bowl and add 2 tbsp tea leaves. Leave to stand for 3 minutes, then strain into another bowl. Press the leaves with a spoon to extract all the juice.

In a small saucepan, mix together the steeped tea and the remaining caster sugar. Bring to the boil and stir until the sugar is dissolved and the syrup is shiny and thickening, or measures 50°C/120°F on a sugar thermometer.

Meanwhile, beat the egg yolks in a bowl until they are thick and lemon-coloured. Pour in the tea syrup little by little, beating constantly, until the mixture has cooled.

In a saucepan, heat 100 ml/4 fl oz cream until it boils, remove from the heat and stir in the remaining tea leaves. Leave to stand for 5 minutes, then strain into a bowl, pressing hard with the back of a spoon to extract all the juice. Whisk together the tea-cream and the egg yolk mixture.

In another bowl, beat the egg whites until they reach soft peaks, then beat in the icing sugar until they become stiff. Fold the meringue into the tea-cream and egg yolk mixture.

In another bowl, beat the remaining cream until it reaches soft peak stage. Fold into the mixture with the pistachios.

Line a 1.25 litre/2¼ pt bombe mould with cling film. Spoon the drained kumquats into the bottom of the bombe mould, pressing up around the sides as far as they will go. Pour the tea-cream mixture into the mould and smooth the top. Freeze for at least 4 hours, or until it is solid.

Meanwhile, make the rum topping. Beat the rum and the sugar until the sugar has dissolved. Add the cream and continue to beat until the mixture has thickened. Serve the unmoulded ice cream with the rum sauce.

SOFT SWEET CHEESE PANCAKES

TVOROZHNIKI

◆ ◆ ◆

These hand-formed pancakes are sometimes served for breakfast in the better Moscow and St Petersburg hotels. The constituents bear a distinct resemblance to the fillings you will find in later chapters – the combination of lemon rind, eggs and cheese is a favourite throughout Eastern Europe and Western Russia.

SERVES 4–6

- ◆ *50 g/2 oz plain flour*
- ◆ *450 g/1 lb curd cheese*
- ◆ *1 large egg*
- ◆ *salt*
- ◆ *1 tbsp sugar*
- ◆ *½ tsp vanilla essence*
- ◆ *grated rind of 1 small lemon*
- ◆ *flour*
- ◆ *40–50 g/1½–2 oz butter*
- ◆ *sour cream (optional)*
- ◆ *fresh fruit – apricots, peaches, raspberries, as desired (optional)*

Sieve the flour into a large bowl, then force the curd cheese through the same sieve into the bowl. Add the egg, a pinch of salt, the sugar, vanilla essence and lemon rind. Stir to mix well.

Transfer the mixture to a floured board and form into 12 small patties. Arrange on a plate, cover with cling film, and chill for 2–24 hours.

Before cooking, dredge the patties in flour, brushing off the excess. Melt the butter in a frying pan and cook the *tvorzhniki* until they are golden brown on both sides. Serve warm with sour cream, and fresh soft fruit, peeled and sliced, if desired.

2

FROM RUSSIA'S HEARTLAND
The Russian Federation

————

The newly christened Russian Federation encompasses the same vast area once known as the Russian Republic. Its vertical expanse stretches from the icy permafrost of arctic Siberia to the southern shores of lake Baikal. A crow flying east to west would cross five time zones.

'If we have bread and *kvas* what more do we need?' So says the anonymous peasant of Russian folklore. This was likely to have been a stoical acceptance of the poor man's lot rather than an out-of-hand rejection of improvement, since the chances of much else in medieval to 19th-century Russia were limited.

Bread was the staple, served up in black, brown or white doorsteps and also used in stuffings, soups and, together with barley or rye flour, as the basis for *kvas* (near beer), an invention of the early Slavs.

Some trademarks of European Russian cuisine had come with the invasion of the Tartars – sour cream and curd cheese, fruit relishes and conserves, cucumbers and cabbage preserved in brine, and tea. In general, however, medieval to 19th-century peasant cuisine evolved around the need to cook with very little or no meat – for the most part a luxury reserved for Orthodox feast days.

In addition to wheat and rye flour breads – often eaten with cloves of garlic and coarse salt – the countryman's larder relied on grains and vegetables which would survive the long winters in earth cellars or on the shelf: salted or pickled cabbage, swedes, buckwheat flour and groats (*kasha*), barley (*yachmyer*), millet (*prosso*), onions, beetroot and potatoes – the latter brought to Russia at the instigation of Peter the Great. Fresh items might include eggs, sour cream (*smetana*), homemade pot cheese, wild soft fruits and mushrooms. These last are still an obsession with Russians today.

PRE-REVOLUTIONARY RUSSIA

With the Great Reforms of the 1860s, serfs were freed, the lot of the small landowner improved and village communes were set up. By the late 19th century, Russia and the Ukraine were exporting wheat to a needy Europe. The physical limitations imposed by the size of the country, the corruption of officialdom and the intransigence of the class system would eventually combine with other political factors to bring about revolution, but for the first time in many homes there was meat in the pot, if only poorer cuts which could be minced or stewed while the better ones went to market. For this reason the Russian tradition of peasant cookery is particularly rich in recipes for leafy vegetables, dumplings and pastries stuffed with meat, as well as for meatballs, patties and rissoles.

TRADITIONAL SOUPS

Perhaps the greatest contribution of the homely Russian cook, however, is the repertoire of wonderful comfort soups originally made to sustain labourers and farmers during the long cold winters, and of light chilled soups devised to bring refreshment in the hottest of humid summers. Many exhibit an idiosyncratic sour tang provided by adding pickles, capers, lemon juice, vinegar, *kvas*, sour cream, sorrel or sauerkraut, while a strongly flavoured meat and vegetable stock acts as a foil. Typically, ingredients too have body – barley or hunks of bread, chunky pieces of potato, beetroot, cabbage and cheaper cuts of meat thicken the broth of winter soups, while finely chopped or puréed vegetables, wild mushrooms – fresh or dried – greens, and, sometimes, fruits form the basis of summer specialities.

Though the grand tradition of cooking – as described in the previous chapter – was evolving into a comfortable bourgeois cuisine by the beginning of the 20th century, the revolution of 1917 brought an end to that. The peasant diet became the only ideologically acceptable one. Of all the Soviet states, it was probably Russia itself which suffered most in its self-imposed gustatory *gulag*.

The wholesome, if basic, Russian peasant cuisine, if treated with respect, could have developed like the cooking traditions of nearby Germany, Poland and Hungary. Certainly its Russo-Slavic foundation was rich in leavening influences even within the republic's borders: from the Cossack, Tartar and Turkic peoples of the lower Volga-Don and northern Transcaucasian regions; from the Karelians (relatives of the Finns) in the north; from the eclectic mixture of indigenous and exiled races in Siberia. But circumstances of history and economics conspired to make that scenario impossible.

PERESTROIKA IN THE KITCHEN

The lack of coherent development strategy in farming and technology, the emphasis on ideology in place of imagination, the stark realities of survival under successive repressive regimes, all meant that cultivated frivolities like cooking and eating well were not, could not, be of interest. In effect, the cookery of European Russia has been on the back burner – with the gas turned off – since 1917. But *perestroika* (restructuring) has come to the kitchen as well, and now almost three quarters of a century of neglect is finally being countered by new interest in foodie capitals abroad, and in the co-operative restaurants springing up in Russian cities. It will take time, but the pride in heritage exhibited by these exclusive establishments will find its way back to a people who can now plan for the future while freely talking of the past.

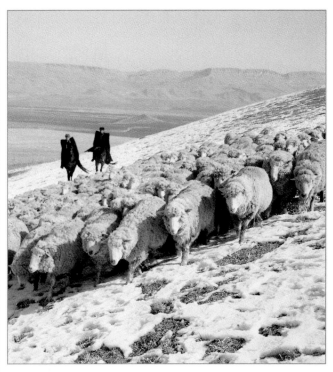

Above: *On the Khabesky state farm, shepherds tend their flock on the northern slope of the Greater Caucasus.*

Far Left: *In a huge commercial greenhouse in the Stavropol region of Russia, a worker sorts red peppers.*

Below: *Harvesting wheat on a collective farm in the Belgorod region of Russia.*

MEAT AND KVAS SOUP

OKROSHKA

◆ ◆ ◆

The kvas can be replaced by flat beer or semi-sweet cider, though the slightly sour flavour of rye will be missing. This dish may be served hot or cold.

SERVES 6–8

- ◆ *2 hard boiled eggs, separated*
- ◆ *2 tsp dry mustard powder*
- ◆ *150 ml/¼ pt sour cream*
- ◆ *salt and freshly ground black pepper*
- ◆ *1.25 litres/2¼ pt kvas, flat beer or cider*
- ◆ *1 medium cucumber, peeled, seeded and finely diced*
- ◆ *2 spring onions, including trimmed green top, finely chopped*
- ◆ *2 medium potatoes, cooked, peeled and finely diced*
- ◆ *225 g/8 oz cold cooked roast beef or pork, finely diced*
- ◆ *large pinch of cayenne pepper*
- ◆ *50 g/2 oz dill or chives, finely chopped*

Finely chop the whites of the eggs and set aside. In a bowl, mash the yolks with the dry mustard powder and a teaspoonful of the sour cream until you have a paste. Then slowly whip in the rest of the sour cream until smooth. Season with 1½–2 tsp salt and pepper to taste.

Whisk in the *kvas*, little by little, until the liquid is thoroughly combined with the sour cream mixture. Stir in the egg whites, cucumber, onions, potatoes, meat and cayenne pepper. Chill for 15 minutes, then ladle into bowls and garnish with chopped dill or chives.

CLASSIC BORSCH

◆ ◆ ◆

To most people borsch is the quintessential Russian dish. It appears in countless variations: clear and chilled for the summer, with a variety of meats in Ukrainian or Moldovan manner, or with the addition of less orthodox ingredients, such as mushrooms or barley.

SERVES 6

- *25–40 g/1–1¹/₂ oz butter*
- *2 beef shins, cut into thin slices*
- *1 large onion, chopped*
- *1 medium turnip, chopped*
- *1 large carrot, sliced*
- *900 g/2 lb fresh beetroot, diced*
- *2 litres/3¹/₂ pt beef stock*
- *60 ml/4 tbsp red wine vinegar*
- *2 bay leaves*
- *1 tsp sugar*
- *salt and freshly ground black pepper*
- *5 sprigs fresh parsley*
- *5 sprigs fresh dill*
- *225 g/8 oz white cabbage, cored and shredded*
- *225 ml/8 fl oz sour cream*

In a large saucepan, melt the butter over medium heat and add the meat, onion, turnip and carrot. Cook briefly, tossing the meat and vegetables, for about 10 minutes, until the meat is browned and the vegetables softened and sweated. Stir in the beetroot and 225 ml/8 fl oz of the beef stock, the vinegar, bay leaves, sugar and seasoning to taste. The soup will need quite a bit of salt to bring out the flavour, so don't be too stingy; about 1¹/₂ tsp should be about right. Cover the pan and simmer the contents for 45 minutes.

Uncover the pan and add the parsley and dill, tied together, and the shredded cabbage, along with the rest of the beef stock. Bring to the boil, then cover and simmer for another 30 minutes.

Before serving, remove the bundle of herbs and the bay leaves. Stir the soup, breaking up the meat and mashing some of the vegetables for a thicker consistency. Serve the soup in warmed bowls and top each with a tablespoon of sour cream.

SOUR BREAD DRINK

KVAS

◆ ◆ ◆

Recipes for this vary slightly in how sweet they are. Start with this slightly tarter recipe and increase the amount of sugar if desired. This is sold by street vendors and taken as a cold drink with meals, but it will probably find more favour with British cooks as an ingredient for cold summer soups.

MAKES ABOUT 3 LITRES/5 PT

- *450 g/1 lb slightly stale black or dark rye bread*
- *3 litres/5 pt boiling water*
- *5 tsp/(2 x 8 g/¹/₄ oz packets) active dry yeast*
- *100 g/4 oz sugar*
- *45 ml/3 tbsp lukewarm water*
- *1 large sprig of mint*
- *sultanas or raisins*

Preheat the oven to 110°C/225°F/Gas Mark ¹/₄. Place the bread in the oven for about 1–1¹/₂ hours, or until it is very dry. *Do not let it burn.* Crumble the bread into a bowl and pour the boiling water over it. Cover with a tea towel and leave for at least 8 hours.

Line a fine sieve with muslin and strain the bread liquid through it into a large bowl, pressing the bread with a spoon to extract as much liquid as possible. Discard the bread.

Sprinkle the yeast and a large pinch of sugar over the lukewarm water and stir to dissolve completely. Set aside in a warm spot for about 10 minutes, or until the mixture is foamy and almost double in volume. Stir the yeast mixture, the rest of the sugar and the mint sprig into the bread water. Cover with a tea towel and set aside for another 8–12 hours.

Strain the liquid again through a muslin-lined sieve placed over a large bowl. Sterilize 5 x 600 ml/1 pt bottles – glass milk bottles will do nicely. Pour the liquid into each bottle until it is about two-thirds full, then drop 4–5 raisins or sultanas in. Cover the tops with cling film secured with a rubber band.

Place the bottles in a cool dark place for about 3 days, until the raisins/sultanas have risen to the top and the sediment sunk to the bottom. Carefully pour off the clear liquid into a bowl, leaving the sediment behind. Thoroughly clean the bottles, remove the raisins/sultanas from the *kvas*, and funnel it back into the bottles (there will be slightly less). Cork the bottles or cover with cling film and refrigerate until ready to use. This will keep for several weeks well-covered in the fridge.

SIBERIAN RAVIOLI

PELMENI

◆ ◆ ◆

Traditionally, *pelmeni* were made in the autumn, with the coming of the first snowfalls. They were frozen, uncooked, in the snow banks outside the house, and hacked off in chunks whenever needed. The fillings used off-cuts of meat, while the dough could be made with or without egg. For fish *pelmeni*, substitute halibut, bream or salmon for the meat, and butter mashed with two hard-boiled egg yolks for the pork fat.

MAKES ABOUT 65–70

- ◆ 225 g/8 oz plain flour
- ◆ salt
- ◆ 1 large egg
- ◆ melted butter (optional)
- ◆ sour cream (optional)

For the filling

- ◆ 175 g/6 oz minced lean beef
- ◆ 100 g/4 oz minced lean pork
- ◆ 50 g/2 oz minced pork fat
- ◆ 1 large onion, finely chopped
- ◆ 1 tsp salt
- ◆ freshly ground black pepper

To make the filling, mix together all the filling ingredients in a large bowl. Set aside.

To make the dough, place the flour and salt in the bowl of a food processor fitted with the metal blade. With the motor running, add the egg, then as much water as is necessary for the dough to just begin to form a ball (about 30–60 ml/2–4 tbsp). Remove the dough to a floured surface. Knead for about 8 minutes or until smooth, flouring the surface as necessary to keep the dough from sticking. Form the dough back into a ball, flatten slightly, and chill it, wrapped in cling film, for about 2 hours.

To make the *pelmeni*, roll out the dough on a lightly floured surface until it is a rectangle about 3 mm/$^1/_8$ in thick. Insert your hands under the dough and begin stretching it by pulling it carefully over the backs of your hands. When it is very thin, spread it on a table. With a knife, trim it into a square or rectangle and cut out 7.5 cm/3 in rounds with a biscuit cutter or lid. Drop a scant 1 tsp of filling on one side of each round. Brush the circular edge all round with a little water and fold over the dough to form a half circle. Seal by pressing the edges with a fork. Wet both ends of the *pelmeni*, bring them round, and pinch together in the shape of an Italian tortellini. Arrange the *pelmeni* on a baking tray, cover with a tea towel, and freeze overnight. (The *pelmeni* may be kept frozen for up to 3 months.)

To cook the *pelmeni*, bring 2 litres/3$^1/_2$ pt water to the boil in a large saucepan. Drop the *pelmeni* in by the dozen, bring back to the boil and reduce to low. Simmer uncovered for about 10 minutes, or until they rise to the surface. Remove with a slotted spoon, drain thoroughly, and bring the water back to the boil. Repeat with the remaining *pelmeni*. Serve with melted butter or sour cream.

PRETZEL-SHAPED SWEET BREAD

KRENDEL

◆ ◆ ◆

This much-loved sweet bread makes a delicious accompaniment to tea drawn from a silver samovar. Given a more cake-like consistency with the addition of more flour and eggs, but retaining the same shape, it is also popular as the centrepiece for a birthday or name-day celebration.

MAKES 1 LOAF

- ◆ 45 ml/3 tbsp luke warm water
- ◆ 2$^1/_2$ tsp (1 x 8 g/$^1/_4$ oz packet) active dry yeast
- ◆ 3 tbsp plus 1 tsp sugar
- ◆ 350 g/12 oz plain flour
- ◆ $^1/_2$ tsp salt
- ◆ 50 g/2 oz unsalted butter
- ◆ 50 g/2 oz slivered blanched almonds
- ◆ 3 standard-size eggs
- ◆ 100 ml/4 fl oz single cream
- ◆ 2 tbsp icing sugar

Place the lukewarm water in a small bowl and sprinkle in the yeast and 1 tsp sugar. Leave for 10 minutes to become foamy and almost double in volume.

Sift 300 g/11 oz of the flour, the remaining sugar and the salt into another bowl. Cut in the butter in small pieces, and work the mixture with your hands until it becomes crumbly. Lightly beat 2 eggs and stir into the flour mixture, followed by the cream and the yeast mixture. Combine thoroughly to make a dough. If the dough is not firm enough sift in the remaining flour, little by little, until the dough is manageable.

Gather the dough into a ball and transfer to a well-floured surface. Knead for about 5 minutes, or until it is smooth and elastic. Reshape into a ball, transfer to a lightly buttered bowl, turning to coat in the butter, cover with a tea towel, and let it rise for 30 minutes or until double in size.

Knock down the dough and, on a floured surface, shape it into a long rope about 5 cm/2 in in diameter. Taper the ends and twist the dough over and under into a pretzel shape.

Preheat the oven to 200°C/400°F/Gas Mark 6. Transfer the dough to a buttered baking tray, cover again with the tea towel and leave to rise in a warm place until it has doubled in size, about 30 minutes. Brush with an egg wash made from beating the remaining egg with a little water, and sprinkle with the almonds.

Bake for 15 minutes then cover with foil and bake for 10–15 minutes more, until the top and almonds are golden. Transfer the bread to a rack and when cool, sprinkle with sifted icing sugar.

Pretzel-shaped Sweet Bread

MARINATED MUSHROOMS

MARINOVANNYE GRIBY

◆ ◆ ◆

In Russia, the Ukraine and the Baltic states, some of the enthusiasm for wild mushrooms is now tempered with fear, since fungi – particularly the thick-stalked *cep* or *boletus* known colloquially as the 'Penny Bun' – have been shown to be severely contaminated by the fallout from Chernobyl. Fortunately our own wild mushrooms, and those available from an increasing number of suppliers, are unaffected.

SERVES 4–6

- ◆ *450 g/1 lb fresh whole button mushrooms, or a mixture of button and oyster mushrooms*
- ◆ *2 cloves garlic*
- ◆ *2 cloves*
- ◆ *1 bay leaf*
- ◆ *sunflower or vegetable oil*
- ◆ *1 tbsp sugar*
- ◆ *2 tsp salt*
- ◆ *225 ml/8 fl oz red wine vinegar*
- ◆ *150 ml/¼ pt water*
- ◆ *3 peppercorns*

Trim the stalks of the mushrooms so that they are flat with the caps and remove any discoloured parts from the oyster mushrooms. Place the garlic, cloves, bay leaf, peppercorns, sugar and salt in an enamelled or stainless steel saucepan and cover with vinegar and water. Bring the liquid to the boil, add the mushrooms and reduce the heat. Simmer uncovered for about 20 minutes, until the mushrooms sink to the bottom. Remove from the heat, take out the garlic, and let the mixture cool.

Pour the mushrooms and their liquid into 600 ml/1 pt jars and pour over just enough oil to create a film on top. Cover with cling film secured with rubber bands and refrigerate for at least 10 days before using. (They should keep for several months if refrigerated.)

MEAT PATTIES WITH SAUCE

BITKI

◆ ◆ ◆

These tasty little patties can be made with either beef or pork – the latter is probably more common in western Russia and the Ukraine. While the recipe offers the option of cranberry jelly as an accompaniment, in its home regions *bitki* would more usually be paired with lingonberries.

SERVES 4–5

- 50 g/2 oz butter
- 1 medium onion, finely chopped
- 700 g/1$\frac{1}{2}$ lb lean minced pork or beef
- 225 g/8 oz lean minced veal
- 50 g/2 oz minced fresh pork fat
- 75 g/3 oz dry breadcrumbs
- 1 large egg, beaten
- salt and freshly ground black pepper
- 75 g/3 oz lard, chicken fat or dripping
- 150 ml/$\frac{1}{4}$ pt sour cream (optional)
- 100 ml/4 fl oz cranberry jelly (optional)

Heat the butter over medium heat and add the onions. Cook, stirring occasionally, until lightly coloured and softened, about 8 minutes. Transfer to a large bowl and add the minced meats, fat, 50 g/2 oz breadcrumbs, egg and seasoning to taste. Work with your hands until all the ingredients are well combined.

Form the *bitki* into 8–10 thick patties. Turn each of the patties over in the remaining breadcrumbs to coat them. Melt half the lard, chicken fat or dripping in a frying pan over high heat. Fry the patties until they are golden brown, about 5 minutes a side. Transfer to a serving dish and keep warm. Repeat with the remaining lard and patties.

Serve the *bitki* in either of two ways: sour cream can be stirred into the frying pan after the patties are finished, warmed through, and then poured over the *bitki*. Alternatively, serve the *bitki* plain, accompanied by a sauceboat of cranberry jelly.

RUSSIAN POTATO SALAD

KARTOPHELNY SALAT PO-RUSSKI

◆ ◆ ◆

This delicious salad incorporates the dressing which has now become internationally known as 'Russian Dressing'.

SERVES 6–8

- 900 g/2 lb new potatoes
- 2 tbsp finely chopped spring onion
- 3 tbsp finely chopped fresh dill
- 6 tbsp finely chopped sweet-sour gherkin
- 6 radishes, thinly sliced
- fresh dill sprigs

For the dressing

- 175 ml/6 fl oz mayonnaise
- $\frac{1}{2}$ tsp Worcestershire sauce
- 23 ml/1$\frac{1}{2}$ tbsp ketchup
- 30 ml/2 tbsp dry white wine
- 5 ml/1 tsp horseradish sauce

Put the potatoes in a large saucepan of water and bring to the boil. Cover, lower the heat and simmer for about 20 – 25 minutes, or until the potatoes are done. Drain and when cool, cut into 5 mm/$\frac{1}{4}$ in slices.

In a small bowl, whisk together the ingredients for the dressing. In a large bowl, assemble the potatoes, onion, dill, gherkin and radishes. Pour the dressing over and toss gently to combine. Transfer the salad to a serving bowl and chill for 30 minutes before serving garnished with the dill sprigs.

LAKE FISH IN MUSTARD SAUCE

OMUL Z ZAPRVKOI GORCHICHINOI

◆ ◆ ◆

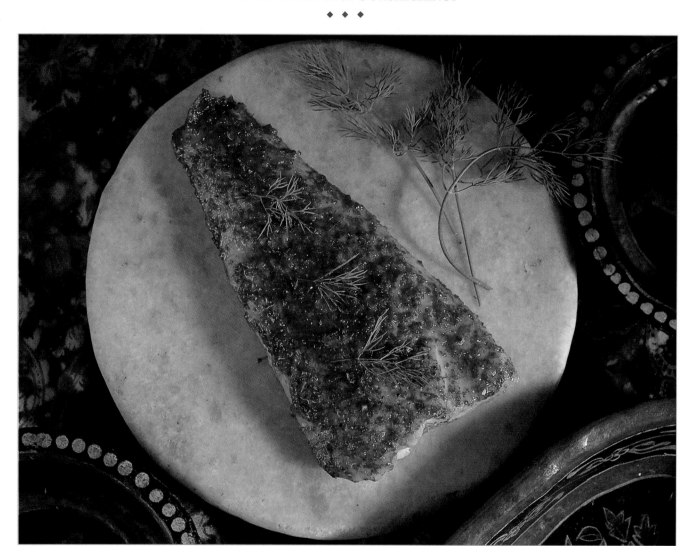

Omul is a delicious relative of the salmon, found only in Siberia's Lake Baikal, one of the most beautiful lakes and on record as the deepest (1.6 km/1 mile) in the world. This recipe would use local wildflower honey and the fish would be baked over an open brushwood fire; here we must be content with ordinary honey, best Scottish salmon and a barbecue or grill.

SERVES 6

- ◆ *30 ml/2 tbsp sunflower oil*
- ◆ *1.5 kg/3 lb salmon fillet, washed and dried*
- ◆ *38 ml/2¹/₂ tbsp German-style mustard*
- ◆ *23 ml/1¹/₂ tbsp honey*
- ◆ *grated rind and juice of ¹/₂ small lemon*
- ◆ *1 tbsp finely chopped fresh dill*
- ◆ *salt and freshly ground black pepper*
- ◆ *dill sprigs*

If you are grilling the fish, brush a sheet of foil with a little sunflower oil before placing the salmon skin-side down on it. Whether grilling or barbecueing, place the fish (and foil, if used) on a baking tray. Mix together the remaining oil, mustard, honey, lemon rind and juice and chopped dill. Brush the fish liberally with the mixture.

Pre-heat a grill to hot. (If you are using a barbecue, the coals should be greying. Place the fish in a fish holder and turn it flesh-side down towards the coals.)

Grill or barbecue the fish about 13 cm/5 in from the heat for about 10 minutes, or until slightly translucent. Transfer to a serving platter and garnish with dill sprigs before serving.

STUFFED CABBAGE ROLLS

GOLUBTSY

◆ ◆ ◆

Cabbage rolls are made by Russians, Poles, Czechs and Hungarians, though each version has special spices and ingredients. The Hungarian one makes use of paprika, while typical recipes from the Ukraine – where they are called *holubsti* – contain mushrooms and are often meatless.

SERVES 8

- 1.25–1.5 kg/2$\frac{1}{2}$–3 lb white Dutch or Savoy cabbage
- 40 g/1$\frac{1}{2}$ oz butter
- 15 ml/1 tbsp oil
- 2 large onions, finely chopped
- 450 g/1 lb minced lean beef
- 225 g/8 oz minced lean veal
- 225 g/8 oz cooked long-grain white rice
- 1 egg, beaten
- salt and freshly ground black pepper
- 6 slices bacon
- 400 g/14 oz can chopped tomatoes
- 100 ml/4 fl oz beef stock
- 1 tbsp flour
- 150 ml/$\frac{1}{4}$ pt sour cream
- 50 g/2 oz fresh dill, finely chopped

Bring a large saucepan or casserole of water to boil. Lower in the whole head of cabbage. Cover and cook for about 8 minutes. Remove the cabbage but keep the water on the boil. Carefully remove as many leaves as you can without tearing them. Return the cabbage to the saucepan and cook for a little longer, then remove and again detach as many leaves as you can. Repeat the process until you have 20 or so large leaves. Trim each leaf, removing the toughest part of the central stalk. Set aside.

In a frying pan, heat the butter and oil and sauté the onion until it is softened and golden. Transfer to a large bowl and add the beef, veal, cooked rice, egg and seasoning to taste. Mix with your hands until thoroughly combined.

Lay 3–4 leaves out and place about 3 tbsp of filling on each. Roll up from the stalk end, turning in the sides, and finish at the leafy end to make a neat packet. If necessary, secure with a wooden cocktail stick. Place the packets seam-side down in a shallow casserole large enough to hold all the rolls in one layer. Lay the bacon slices over the rolls.

Preheat the oven to 180°C/350°F/Gas Mark 4. In a saucepan, heat together the chopped tomatoes and beef stock. Remove 30 ml/2 tbsp to mix with the flour in a bowl. Whisk in the sour cream and dill and return the mixture to the hot tomato-beef stock mixture, stirring. Season to taste and pour the sauce over the cabbage rolls.

Bake the rolls, uncovered, for 1 hour or until the sauce is bubbling and the rolls are slightly browned. Allow to rest for 10 minutes before serving.

HAM SAUSAGE WITH CABBAGE

KOLBASA Z KAPUSTOY

◆ ◆ ◆

Kolbasa is a smoked ham sausage common throughout the European states. Like many processed pork products, it is largely produced for sale in Poland and nearby Ukraine and Belorussia. It can be eaten hot or cold.

SERVES 4–6

- ◆ *1 large head red cabbage, shredded*
- ◆ *25 g/1 oz butter*
- ◆ *75 ml/3 fl oz lemon juice*
- ◆ *100 ml/ 4 fl oz beef stock*
- ◆ *50 ml/2 fl oz red wine*
- ◆ *salt and pepper*
- ◆ *2 tsp brown sugar*
- ◆ *1 tbsp cornflour*
- ◆ *450 g/1 lb kolbasa or other smoked ham sausage, thinly sliced*

Place the shredded cabbage in a colander and pour boiling water over it. Drain thoroughly.

Melt the butter in a heavy flameproof casserole over medium heat. Stir in the cabbage and sauté for 5 minutes. Add the lemon juice and continue stirring for another 5 minutes; the cabbage will be bright pink. Pour over the stock and wine, cover, and lower the heat. Simmer for 45 minutes.

Mix together the sugar and cornflour in a small bowl; stir in a little of the cooking liquid. Stir the mixture into the cabbage and raise the heat to high. Stir as the sauce thickens, then add the sausage. Cover and simmer for 30 minutes. Serve with thick slabs of rye bread.

HAM IN RYE PASTRY

OKOROK V RZHANOM TESTE

◆ ◆ ◆

This is a popular Easter dish which can be served either hot or cold, as here. It would be well partnered by cabbage cooked with sour cream, boiled potatoes with dill, and a pot of German-style mustard. The rather hard, dry pastry can be discarded before serving, if desired; it is really there to seal in the flavour of the spiced ham.

SERVES 10–12

- ◆ *75 g/3 oz dark brown sugar*
- ◆ *1 tsp dry mustard powder*
- ◆ *1/4 tsp ground cloves*
- ◆ *large pinch of ground cinnamon*
- ◆ *2.5 kg/5 lb canned Polish ham*
- ◆ *milk*

For the pastry

- ◆ *2 1/2 tsp (1 x 8 g/1/4 oz packet) active dry yeast*
- ◆ *45 ml/3 tbsp lukewarm water*
- ◆ *50 g/2 oz caraway seeds*
- ◆ *75 ml/6 fl oz water*
- ◆ *30 ml/2 tbsp molasses*
- ◆ *375 g/12 oz rye flour*

Make the pastry first. Dissolve the yeast in lukewarm water in a small bowl. Add the caraway seeds and set aside in a warm place for 10 minutes to become foamy and double in volume.

Stir in 175 ml/6 fl oz cold water, the molasses and half the flour, a little at a time. Take the resultant dough out of the bowl and place on a floured surface. Knead in the remaining flour, little by little. The dough should be stiff. Cover with cling film and set aside for 30 minutes. Meanwhile, remove the aspic from the ham and pat the ham dry with absorbent kitchen paper.

Roll out the dough to form a 66 x 25 cm/26 x 10 in rectangle. Mix together the sugar, mustard, cloves and cinnamon in a small bowl. Sprinkle a heaped tbsp of the mixture in the centre of the dough. Place the ham on top and pat the remaining mixture over the ham.

Preheat the oven to 180°C/350°F/Gas Mark 4. Fold the dough neatly over the ham, tucking the corners in and sealing it where the edges meet with a little water. Set the ham on a foil-lined baking tray, brush with milk, and bake for 1 3/4–2 hours. Remove from the oven and allow to rest for 15 minutes before slicing the ham (and removing the pastry surround, if desired).

Ham Sausage with Cabbage

DEEP-FRIED BUTTER TWISTS

KHVOROST

◆ ◆ ◆

**These are among the most beloved of Russian
biscuits. They are a happy reminder of childhood
to many Russian immigrants around the world.**

MAKES ABOUT 25–30

- *1 large egg*
- *4 large egg yolks*
- *4 tbsp icing sugar*
- *30 ml/2 tbsp rum*
- *5 ml/1 tsp vanilla essence*
- *1/2 tsp salt*
- *185 g/6 1/2 oz plain flour*
- *oil or fat*
- *icing sugar, or
  combination of caster
  sugar and ground
  cinnamon*

In a large bowl, use an electric mixer to beat the egg and egg
yolks with the sugar until the mixture is thick and fluffy –
about 10 minutes. Stir in the rum, vanilla essence and salt.

Sift the flour into the bowl little by little, stirring after each
addition. By the time you have added 6 1/2 oz, you should have
a stiff paste; turn it out on to a floured surface. Knead the
dough on a floured surface until smooth and elastic – about
10 minutes. Divide the dough in half and cover half with a
damp towel.

Roll out the dough as thinly as possible and cut into
13 x 5 cm/5 x 2 in strips. Make a slit from the centre almost to
the end of one strip and thread the other end through the
slit. Repeat with the remaining strips. Roll out the remaining
dough and repeat the process.

Heat the oil or fat in a deep-fryer or large saucepan until
water-spit hot and deep-fry the *khvorost* turning once or twice,
in batches, until golden. Drain the twists on paper towels
before sprinkling with cinnamon or icing sugar.

SWEET POT-CHEESE TARTLETS

VATRUSHKI

◆ ◆ ◆

Vatrushki **are served as a savoury** *zakuska,* **as a sweet to go with tea, as here, or as a large dessert tart.**

MAKES ABOUT 16 TARTLETS

- ◆ *200 g/7 oz plain flour*
- ◆ *1/2 tsp baking powder*
- ◆ *50 g /2 oz sugar*
- ◆ *pinch of salt*

- ◆ *1 large egg*
- ◆ *90 ml/3 fl oz sour cream*
- ◆ *65 g/2 1/2 oz unsalted butter*

For the filling

- ◆ *50 ml/2 fl oz rum*
- ◆ *30ml/2tbsp water*
- ◆ *75 g/3 oz raisins*
- ◆ *500 g/18 oz cottage cheese*
- ◆ *4 eggs*
- ◆ *175 g/6 oz sugar*

- ◆ *2 tsp grated lemon rind*
- ◆ *100 g/4 oz clarified butter, melted*
- ◆ *1/4 tsp salt*
- ◆ *50 g/2 oz flour*

Make the filling first. Heat the rum and 30 ml /2 tbsp water in a saucepan over high heat until almost boiling. Remove from the heat and stir in the raisins. Set aside.

Line a colander with muslin and pour in the cottage cheese. Leave to drain for 3 hours.

In a large bowl, beat the cottage cheese using an electric mixer. Beat in the eggs, one at a time, and the sugar, until the mixture is pale in colour. Stir in the lemon rind, melted butter, salt and flour, 1 tbsp at a time. Drain the raisins, discard the liquid and fold the raisins into the cottage cheese.

To make the dough, sift the flour, baking powder, sugar and salt into a large bowl. Beat the egg and sour cream in a small bowl. Make a well in the centre of the flour and pour the egg mixture into it. With your hands, slowly work the flour into the liquid, then beat until the mixture forms a ball. Wrap in cling film and chill for 1 hour.

Preheat the oven to 200°C/400°F/Gas Mark 6. On a well floured surface, roll the dough out into a rectangle as thinly as possible. Cut out 16 or so 10 cm/4 in rounds from the dough, gathering and re-rolling the scraps as necessary. Make a rim around each circle by folding over and pinching up the dough, so that you end up with shallow tartlet cases.

Place the cases on a greased baking tray and spoon some of the filling into each case. Bake for 15–20 minutes, or until the *vatrushki* are golden. Remove and cool on a wire rack.

WHIPPED EGGS AND SUGAR

GOGOL MOGOL

◆ ◆ ◆

**This is Russian *zabaglione*, simple as that!
A timeless dessert, made in kitchens all over Russia.**

SERVES 2–3

◆ *6 egg yolks* ◆ *75 g/3 oz sugar*
◆ *30 ml/2 tbsp rum*

Beat the sugar with the egg yolk until foamy and pale lemon in colour. Stir in the rum. Pour the mixture into tall glasses and serve with thin Belgian-style butter twists or *khvorost*.

EASTER CAKE

KULICH

◆ ◆ ◆

**This is the traditional festive Easter cake.
Some recipes include curd cheese to give it a thicker,
pastier consistency.**

SERVES 8–10

- 2¹/₂ tbsp (3 x 8g/¹/₄ oz
  packets) active dry yeast
- 225 g/8 oz plus 1 tsp sugar
- 10 ml/2 tsp water
- 75 g/3 oz sultanas
- 50ml/2 fl oz rum
- 300ml/¹/₂ pt lukewarm milk
- 575–625 g/20–22 oz flour
- ¹/₂ tsp powdered saffron
- 3 eggs
- 2 egg yolks
- 5 ml/1 tsp vanilla essence
- 100 g/4 oz unsalted
  butter, cut into small pieces
- 75 g/3 oz mixed peel
- 50 g/2 oz slivered
  almonds, toasted
- 2 cardomom seeds, crushed
  to powder
- flour

For the glaze
- 275 g/10 oz icing sugar
- 10 ml/2 tsp red wine
- 35 ml/7 tsp water

Mix the yeast and 1 tsp sugar with the water to make a paste. Soak the sultanas in the rum for at least 15 minutes.

Stir the lukewarm milk into the yeast paste, and beat in about 225 g/8 oz of the flour, until you have a thin batter. Cover and leave in a warm place for 30 minutes to double in volume and become frothy.

Drain the sultanas, reserving the liquid and pat them dry with kitchen paper. Add the saffron to the rum and set aside.

Sift the remaining sugar and flour, a little at a time, into the frothy mixture, until you have a stiff batter. Beat the eggs and the egg yolks one at a time into the dough, together with the vanilla essence, kneading with your hands when it becomes possible. Work the butter into the dough little by little

Pour the saffron and rum over the dough and knead in. Make the dough into a ball and transfer to a floured surface. Knead hard with the heel of your hand, turning and pulling, for about 10 minutes. If necessary, knead in more flour to make sure the dough does not stick. When the dough is shiny and smooth, make into a ball again. Dust with flour and place in a buttered bowl.

Leave to stand in a warm place for 1 hour or until the dough has doubled in size.

Toss the mixed peel, slivered almonds and the soaked and drained sultanas in a bowl with 1 tbsp flour and the crushed cardomom. Knock down the dough in the bowl. Add a little of the mixed fruit and knead in; continue until all the fruit is evenly taken in by the dough. Leave the dough in the bowl, cover and put in a warm place for 1 hour to rise again.

Butter a deep cylindrical tin – an empty 900 g/2 lb coffee or powdered milk tin will do – and line with a buttered piece of greaseproof paper. When the dough has doubled in size again, knock it down and transfer it to the tin.

Preheat the oven to 200°C/400°F/Gas Mark 6. Leave the dough to rise until it almost reaches the top of the tin. Bake for 15 minutes, then lower the heat to 180°C/350°F/Gas Mark 4 and bake for a further hour, or until the puffed top has turned golden.

Cool in the tin on a wire rack for 10 minutes then lift carefully, turn out the cake and cover with a towel. Make the glaze. In a bowl, beat together the icing sugar, water and red wine with a wooden spoon, until thoroughly combined. Uncover the cake and pour the glaze over it.

Serve by cleanly cutting off the crown and reserving it to be eaten last, then cutting the cake in half vertically and cutting each half into half-circle slices.

3

LOOKING WESTWARD FROM THE BALTIC

Estonia, Latvia and Lithuania

———

The political events of the last five to six years have brought three small states dramatically into the public eye — three states which many in the West could hardly locate on a map, much less arrange in order from the north down their jagged stretch of Baltic coastline.

This solemn liturgy at Phyti convent is being officiated by Metropolitan Alexiy, who heads 84 Russian Orthodox parishes in Estonia.

Estonia, Latvia and Lithuania have a common history of subjugation and exploitation by its stronger neighbours. These exploiters have included, in varying permutations, Russia, Germany, Denmark and Sweden, though Lithuania enjoyed a period of influence and independence with her own Duchy, later brought into a Polish-Lithuanian Commonwealth. All fell in the end, however, to the great Russian bear. The repeated submergence of national identity under a foreign yoke, and their final domination by the Soviet Union, has left its mark on the culinary character of all three countries. At the same time, their fierce desire for liberation, which put them in the vanguard of the new independent order, has ensured that some individual characteristics have managed to survive.

The aspects they share have, not surprisingly, been dictated by their location flanking the sea, by their rich agricultural land – making them great producers of barley, oatmeal and rye – and by their proximity to, and dependence on, the old Soviet Union. Buckwheat (*kasha*) is a staple, and Russian-style dishes like stuffed cabbage, meatballs and minced meat cutlets feature prominently. The love of honey which distinguishes much of the former western and southern Soviet states is echoed here, as is the ubiquitous use of sour cream.

Estonia, the most northerly, exhibits a character somewhat apart from its two neighbours. Unlike the Latvians and Lithuanians, Estonians trace their roots to the Finno-Ugric nation and hence share more cultural, linguistic and even gastronomic links with the Finns. In addition, the large numbers of Finnish tourists who have always treated the charming Estonian capital, Tallinn, as a long-weekend playground (the ferry from Helsinki takes only four hours) have now grown to a flood, so that the links with that country are ever-growing. Both the variety of smoked and salted fish, and the occasions demanding its appearance, are evocative of Scandinavia, while Finnish specialities like Queen's Cake are served in Tallinn's coffee houses (*korviks*) and cafés. Caraway is the dominant flavouring, and *Viru Valge*, a brand of local vodka, shares with Scandinavian versions a reputation among connoisseurs for exceptional quality.

Latvia, like Estonia, has an almost Viennese appreciation of coffee, and of the pastries to go with it. Its fishing industry, one of the world's richest during the independent years between the wars, was afterwards commandeered by the Soviets to feed the Russian heartland. This meant that its wealth of sea and freshwater fish was largely unavailable to the local people, and thus much of its fine heritage of recipes for fresh and smoked fish have long been unappreciated. Its dairy farmers fared somewhat better, and thickly whipped cream, sour cream and sour milk figure particularly strongly in Latvian cooking. So too do fresh berries – raspberries, cranberries, red- and blackcurrants, whortleberries (wild blueberries) – made into preserves, baked into pastries and puréed into *kisels*. Fruits such as apple, plum and grape are transformed into drinks called *kosteili*.

Lithuania, the most westernized of the three, is ironically the most Russian in culinary terms. Garlic is as important there as it is in the Ukraine and the Russian Republic, while Lithuanian sausages – particularly a pork and beef version called *sviezia desra* – are reputed to be the most flavourful in Eastern Europe. Both the potato and apple are treated with special respect; mashed, grated, in dumplings and pastry, the former appears in everything from soups to desserts, while the latter features in sweet biscuits, fritters, tarts, cakes, sauces and candy, as well as combining with potatoes in a savoury pudding.

Today all three states are independent, broken free of involvement even in the loose union of the CIS. This resurrection from national death has awoken a deep and emotional pride in their past; repercussions in the already bustling restaurant and café scenes of Tallinn, Riga and Vilnius cannot be far behind.

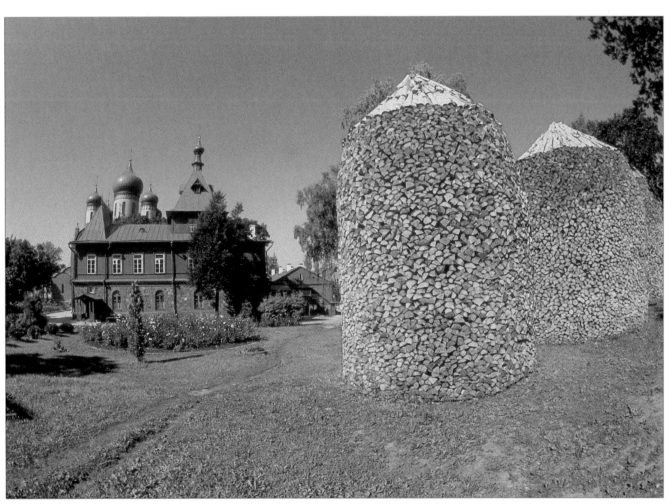

This artfully arranged pile of firewood, at the Phyti Russian Orthodox convent in Estonia,
is as tall as a three-storey building. The birch logs are used in fireplaces for heating and as
kindling in the cooking stoves.

RASPBERRY SOUP

MALINOVYI SUP

◆ ◆ ◆

This is a favourite summer soup of Estonia, and indeed of other Baltic and Eastern European states. It is considered a speciality by the restaurants of Tallinn, Estonia's capital. In season, whortleberries – wild blueberries – can be substituted.

SERVES 6

- ◆ 675 g/1¹/₂ lb raspberries or blueberries
- ◆ 175 g/ 6 oz redcurrants
- ◆ 450 ml/³/₄ pt water
- ◆ 1 tbsp cornflour
- ◆ juice and rind of ¹/₂ lemon
- ◆ 100–150 g/4–5 oz light brown sugar
- ◆ ¹/₂ tsp cinnamon
- ◆ 275 ml/10 fl oz whipping cream
- ◆ 150 ml/¹/₄ pt sour cream

Reserve a large handful of berries for garnish. Place the remainder in a liquidizer or processor fitted with the metal blade and process until the berries are liquified.

Place a fine sieve over an enamelled or stainless-steel saucepan. Press the puréed fruit to extract the seeds, stirring through the sieve in batches until all the liquid has passed through.

Add the water to the strained fruit. Place over high heat and bring to the boil; lower the heat and simmer for 15 minutes. In a small bowl, mix the cornflour with a little water. Whisk into the soup, turn up the heat, and continue whisking as the soup begins to boil and the soup thickens. Lower the heat and whisk in the lemon juice and rind, sugar and cinnamon.

Take off the heat, allow to cool, then chill for several hours or overnight.

Before serving, whisk in the whipping and sour creams. Ladle into individual soup bowls and garnish each with some of the reserved berries.

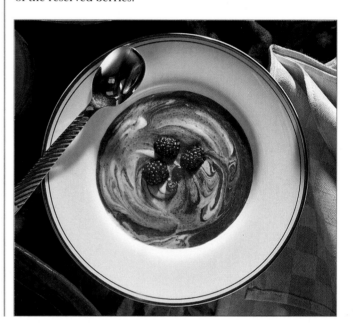

SOUR MILK AND BARLEY SOUP

SKABA PUTRA

◆ ◆ ◆

This is a very old recipe, handed down through generations and still popular today. It is a cold summer soup, for that surprisingly warm season. The coastal strip of Latvia is lapped by the northeasterly waves of the Gulf Stream, making the climate slightly milder than that of its Scandinavian neighbours.

SERVES 6

- ◆ 450 g/1 lb field or brown mushrooms, finely sliced then chopped
- ◆ 50 ml/2 fl oz vegetable oil
- ◆ 1 large onion, finely chopped
- ◆ 1¹/₂ tbsp tomato purée
- ◆ 30 ml/2 tbsp fresh lemon juice
- ◆ 2 litres/3¹/₂ pt chicken stock
- ◆ 225 g/8 oz pearl barley
- ◆ salt and freshly ground black pepper
- ◆ 225 ml/8 fl oz buttermilk
- ◆ 225 ml/8 fl oz sour cream
- ◆ 3 tbsp finely chopped fresh dill
- ◆ 2 hard-boiled eggs, chopped
- ◆ 1 Polish-style sweet-sour pickle, finely chopped

In a large saucepan, sauté the mushrooms in the oil over medium-high heat. Stir until the mushroom juices have evaporated, about 15 minutes. Add the onion and stir until softened, about 8 minutes. Stir in the tomato purée, lemon juice and chicken stock and bring to the boil over high heat.

Slowly stir in the barley and seasoning to taste. Bring back to the boil, cover, and lower the heat. Simmer until the barley is tender, about 30–40 minutes.

Take the soup off the heat and leave to cool. When it is at room temperature, stir in the buttermilk, sour cream and dill. Taste and adjust the seasoning. Chill for at least 1 hour (or overnight, covered) before serving.

Ladle the soup into individual serving bowls and garnish each with the chopped egg and gherkin.

HONEY VODKA

KRUPNIKAS

◆ ◆ ◆

Honey is used as a sweetening agent in all of the Baltic countries, but it is perhaps in Lithuania that it reaches its apogee. *Midus* (mead) is one warming honey-based alcoholic beverage, another is homemade 'fire' or honey vodka.

MAKES ABOUT 900 ML/1 ½ PT

- ◆ *1 vanilla bean*
- ◆ *large pinch nutmeg*
- ◆ *4 strips lemon peel*
- ◆ *175 ml/6 fl oz water*
- ◆ *7 sticks cinnamon*
- ◆ *3 whole cloves*
- ◆ *350 ml/12 fl oz honey*
- ◆ *700 ml/1¹/₄ pt vodka*

In a large saucepan, combine the vanilla bean, nutmeg, cinnamon, cloves, lemon peel and water. Bring the water to the boil and stir in the honey. Bring back to the boil, cover and simmer for 5 minutes.

Remove from the heat and stir in the vodka. The *krupnikas* can be served hot or allowed to cool and then bottled.

Lithuanian Cottage Cheese Bacon Bread

LITHUANIAN COTTAGE CHEESE BACON BREAD

LITOVSKY TWOROZHNY KHLEB Z BECONOM

◆ ◆ ◆

Varske – cottage cheese – and honey are commonly used
as a baking ingredient in Lithuania. This recipe mixes
wholemeal and white flour to give a hint of the sturdier
type of bread you will find in the Baltic States.

MAKES 1 LOAF WEIGHT

- 50 ml/2 fl oz vegetable oil
- 175 g/6 oz lean bacon, finely chopped
- 2 heaped tbsp finely chopped spring onion
- 50 ml/2 fl oz honey
- 175 ml/6 fl oz milk
- 1 egg
- 175 g/ 6 oz cottage cheese
- 150 g/5 oz wholewheat flour
- 150 g/5 oz strong white flour
- 2 tsp baking powder
- 1/2 tsp baking soda
- scant tsp salt

In a small saucepan, heat the vegetable oil over medium-high heat. Add the bacon and fry for a few minutes, until the bacon is cooked. Turn down the heat and stir in the spring onion, allowing it to wilt slightly. Then add the honey, heat through, and remove from the hob. Beat in the milk, egg, and then the cottage cheese. Blend thoroughly and set aside.

In a large bowl, sift together the two flours, baking powder and soda and the salt. Make a well and pour in the cottage cheese mixture, beating gently – do not overbeat.

Preheat the oven to 190°C/375°F/Gas Mark 5. Scrape the bread dough into a buttered and floured 9 x 5 x 3 in loaf tin. Flatten the top of the loaf with a spatula and drop the loaf sharply twice on a hard surface to eliminate air pockets. Bake for 45–50 minutes, or until the top is golden brown.

Place the tin on a wire rack to cool for 15 minutes before turning out. Cool completely before serving.

BARLEY BREAD

YACHMENNY KHLEB

◆ ◆ ◆

Barley bread is made from Finland to the Ukraine and it
makes a change from the black and coarse rye breads which
otherwise predominate in the countryside. In this Estonian
recipe, honey is used to provide a touch of sweetness.

MAKES 2 ROUND LOAVES

- 2 1/2 tsp (1 x 8 g/1/4 oz packet) active dry yeast
- 50 ml/2 fl oz honey
- 100 ml/4 fl oz lukewarm water
- 350 g/12 oz cracked barley
- 175 g/6 oz wholewheat flour
- 2 tsp salt
- 350 ml/12 fl oz lukewarm milk
- 30 ml/2 tbsp vegetable oil
- 175 g/12 oz strong white flour
- 1 egg
- 15 ml/1 tbsp water

Dissolve the yeast, together with 15 ml/1 tbsp honey, in the lukewarm water in a small bowl. Cover the bowl and place it in a warm place for 20 minutes or until foamy and almost doubled in volume.

Meanwhile, in a blender or food processor fitted with the metal blade, grind the barley in batches as finely as possible.

Transfer to a large bowl and add the wholewheat flour and salt. Slowly beat in the yeast mixture, the remaining honey, the lukewarm milk and the oil. Add as much of the white flour as is needed to make a soft, malleable dough. Remove the dough to a floured surface, and, adding a little more white flour all the time, knead until it is shiny and elastic, about 10 minutes. Remove to an oiled bowl, cover with a tea towel and allow to rise in a warm place for 1 hour, or until doubled in size.

Knock down the dough, knead for another 5 minutes and form into two round loaves. Place them on a lightly greased baking sheet and leave them, covered, for another hour, or until well risen.

Preheat the oven to 200°C/400°F/Gas Mark 6. Make an egg wash by beating the egg with the water. Brush the loaves with the wash, prick the tops with a fork and bake for 15 minutes. Lower the heat to 180°C/350°F/Gas Mark 4 and continue baking for a further 30–35 minutes, or until the loaves sound hollow when tapped on the bottom. Cool the bread on wire racks and serve with unsalted butter.

VEGETABLES

POTATO AND APPLE PUDDING

PUDDING IZ KARTOPHELYA I YABLOK

◆ ◆ ◆

In addition to potatoes, apples are another of Lithuania's passions, and they appear in everything from desserts to first courses with herring. This pudding also has variations in Denmark and Germany, where there is a predilection for sweet-savoury combinations. It goes particularly well with pork, goose and duck.

SERVES 4–6

◆ *450 g/1 lb floury potatoes,*
 unpeeled
◆ *¹/₄ tsp nutmeg*
◆ *175 ml/6 fl oz milk*
◆ *450 g/1 lb tart apples, peeled*
◆ *100 g/4 oz butter*
◆ *2 tsp sugar*
◆ *50 ml/2 fl oz double*
 cream
◆ *25 g/ 1 oz breadcrumbs*

In a large saucepan cover the potatoes with water and bring to the boil. Lower the heat and simmer until the potatoes are tender. Meanwhile, in another large saucepan, sauté the apples in 75 g/3 oz butter until softened. Toss the hot apples with the sugar and nutmeg and set aside.

Drain the potatoes and peel while still hot. Mash them with the milk until as smooth as possible. Add the apples in their butter, and the cream. Mash and beat vigorously to combine.

Preheat the oven to 200°C/400°F/Gas Mark 6. Transfer the mixture to a baking dish. Scatter the breadcrumbs over and dot with the remaining butter. Bake for 25 minutes, until the top is golden.

GRATED POTATO AND EGG PUDDING

KUGELIS

◆ ◆ ◆

This is perhaps Lithuania's best-known dish. It is often served with a scattering of separately fried onions on top, but that does seem to be gilding the lily.

SERVES 4–6

- ◆ *1 kg/2 lb baking potatoes, peeled and grated*
- ◆ *1 tsp salt*
- ◆ *2 small eggs*
- ◆ *2 tbsp potato starch or plain flour*
- ◆ *1/2 tsp baking powder*
- ◆ *30 ml/2 tbsp melted bacon fat*
- ◆ *1 small onion, grated*
- ◆ *1/2 tsp caraway seed crushed*
- ◆ *1/4 tsp pepper*
- ◆ *50 g/2 oz butter, melted*

Toss the grated potatoes in a colander with the salt. Drain for 10 minutes then, with your hands, squeeze out as much liquid as possible and pat dry with absorbent kitchen paper.

Beat the eggs in a large bowl. Sift in the potato starch or flour and baking powder and stir in the bacon fat, grated onion, caraway seed and pepper. Add the potatoes and toss well to combine.

Preheat the oven to 180°C/350°F/Gas Mark 4. Transfer the potatoes to a greased baking dish, smooth top, and pour the melted butter over. Bake the potatoes for 35 minutes, then increase the heat to 200°C/400°F/Gas Mark 6 and bake for a further 20 minutes, or until the top is golden brown. Serve immediately.

MEAT AND MUSHROOM PATTIES IN SAUCE

KURZEMES

◆ ◆ ◆

This, together with *ligzdinas* – meatballs stuffed with hard-boiled eggs – is Latvia's best-known main course. Neither is a subtle dish, but they appeal to hearty appetites gained from working in the open air.

SERVES 6

- ◆ *30 ml/2 tbsp vegetable oil*
- ◆ *25 g/1 oz butter*
- ◆ *2 onions, finely chopped*
- ◆ *100 g/4 oz mushrooms*
- ◆ *225 g/8 oz minced pork*
- ◆ *225 g/8 oz minced veal*
- ◆ *100 g/4 oz minced ham*
- ◆ *3 tbsp finely chopped fresh parsley*
- ◆ *1/4 tsp dried thyme*
- ◆ *salt and freshly ground black pepper*
- ◆ *2 tbsp dry breadcrumbs*
- ◆ *1 egg*
- ◆ *175 ml/6 fl oz beef consommé or stock*
- ◆ *150 ml/1/4 pt sour cream*

Melt half the oil and butter in a frying pan over medium heat. Add the onions and sauté gently for about 6 minutes, or until they are just softened. With a slotted spoon, remove half the onions and set aside. Add the mushrooms to the pan and continue cooking until they are very limp and most of the liquid has disappeared from the pan.

In a bowl, combine the three meats with the parsley, thyme and salt and pepper to taste, and the mushrooms and onions from the pan. Use your hands to mix thoroughly, then add the breadcrumbs and egg and continue to combine well. Shape the mixture into 6 patties and flatten them.

Add the remaining oil and butter to the pan. Melt over medium-high heat and sauté the patties until the meat is browned on both sides, about 15 minutes. Pour over consommé or stock, together with the reserved onions, and cook over high heat until the liquid is reduced by half. Reduce the heat to low and remove the patties to a serving dish; keep warm. Stir the sour cream into the sauce and pour over the patties. Serve immediately.

ONION-AND-MUSTARD HERRINGS

SIPOLI MERCE

◆ ◆ ◆

Onions and mustard appear in combination with herring in several Baltic recipes; sometimes the fish is in the sauce, as in Lithuanian *silke cepts*. In this Latvian version, the marriage is a bit more subtle.

SERVES 4

- ◆ *675 g/1¹/₂ lb fresh small herring, gutted, head, backbone and bones removed, washed and patted dry*
- ◆ *8 tbsp rye flour*
- ◆ *50 g/2 oz unsalted butter*
- ◆ *1 medium red onion, peeled, sliced and separated into rings*
- ◆ *2 tbsp finely chopped parsley*
- ◆ *lemon quarters*

For the coating

- ◆ *60 ml/4 tbsp German-style mustard*
- ◆ *15 ml/1 tbsp French-style mustard*
- ◆ *3 small egg yolks*
- ◆ *75 ml/3 fl oz double cream*
- ◆ *salt and freshly ground black pepper*

To make the coating mixture, mix together the two mustards in a small bowl. Whisk in the egg yolks, one by one, then the cream. Season to taste and whisk lightly again.

Spread out one herring on a flat plate. Spoon a little of the coating over the inside of the fish, fold together, and brush the skin on both sides with the mixture. Push to one side of the plate and continue with each of the remaining fish. Use any remaining mixture to recoat the fish. Cover with foil and leave overnight in the refrigerator.

Spread the rye flour on a plate and dip each of the fish into it. Melt the butter in a large frying pan over medium heat. Fry the fish in batches, turning to cook both sides, until they are golden brown, about 6 minutes. Keep warm until all the fish are cooked.

Arrange the fish attractively on a serving dish, with the onion rings and parsley scattered over them. Serve garnished with lemon quarters.

BEETROOT AND TOPS WITH SWEET-SOUR DRESSING

SVYOKLA Z KISLO-SLADKOY PRIPRAVOY

◆ ◆ ◆

A Lithuanian treatment for beetroot. If the stalks and greens are unavailable, use half the dressing on the beetroot and reserve the rest; it can be used to dress a celery and potato salad or carrot salad.

SERVES 6

- ◆ *1.5 kg/2 lb small-to-medium fresh beetroot with tops*

For the dressing

- ◆ *1 tsp dry mustard powder*
- ◆ *3 tbsp sugar*
- ◆ *23 ml/1¹/₂ tbsp honey*
- ◆ *15 ml/1 tbsp fresh lemon juice*
- ◆ *100 ml/ 4 fl oz white wine vinegar*
- ◆ *large pinch of paprika*
- ◆ *1 tsp caraway seeds*
- ◆ *100 ml/4 fl oz vegetable oil*
- ◆ *2 tbsp finely chopped spring onion*

To make the dressing combine all the dressing ingredients except the oil and spring onion in a bowl or blender. Whisk or process until combined, then add the oil in a steady stream, whisking (or running the motor) until the dressing is emulsified. Stir in the spring onion and set aside.

Scrub the beetroot clean and cut off the greens to about 2.5 cm/1 in from the top. Put the beetroot in a large stainless steel or enamelled saucepan and cover with water. Place over high heat, cover and bring to the boil. Lower the heat and simmer for about 15 minutes or until tender. Drain, allow to cool slightly, and slip off the skins.

Trim the stalks from the leafy green tops; wash and drain both separately. Chop the stalks into small pieces, place in another large saucepan, and add just enough water in which to steam them. Bring to the boil, cover, and simmer for about 5 minutes. Meanwhile, shred the greens; add them to the stalks and continue to cook until the green are wilted, about 3 minutes. Drain the greens thoroughly.

Cut off, and discard, the top ends of the beetroot and cut the beetroot into thin slices. In a bowl, toss in half the dressing. In another bowl, place the drained stalks and greens and toss with the remainder of the dressing. Chill both in the refrigerator for at least 2 hours before serving.

Transfer to a serving dish with two compartments or, alternatively, arrange the greens in the centre of a serving plate and surround with the sliced beetroot.

HERRING, MEAT AND BEETROOT SALAD

ROSSOLYE

◆ ◆ ◆

Rossolye is a signature dish of Estonian cuisine, rather like *borsch* is of Russian. It is no surprise that both are based on beetroot. *Rossolye* is a common component of the Estonian version of the *zakuska* table and makes a delicious luncheon dish on a warm summer's day.

SERVES 8

- ◆ *3 tsp dry mustard powder*
- ◆ *¹/₂ tsp sugar*
- ◆ *300 ml/¹/₂ pt whipping cream*
- ◆ *5 large boiled beetroot, peeled and diced*
- ◆ *2 tart apples, cored, peeled and diced*
- ◆ *2 fillets of pickled herring, drained and diced*
- ◆ *450 g/1 lb leftover lean cooked beef or pork, trimmed and diced*
- ◆ *salt and freshly ground black pepper*
- ◆ *6 large potatoes, boiled, peeled and diced*
- ◆ *2 sweet-sour Polish-style chopped gherkins, diced*
- ◆ *30–45 ml/2–3 tbsp dry white wine*
- ◆ *2 hard-boiled eggs, chopped*
- ◆ *lettuce leaves*

To make the dressing, combine the mustard, sugar and whipping cream in a large bowl. By hand or with an electric mixer, whip the mustard cream until it holds soft peaks. Set aside.

In another large bowl, combine the beetroot, apples, potatoes, gherkins, herrings, meat, seasoning to taste, and the wine. Toss to combine. Then gently fold in the hard-boiled eggs and three-quarters of the dressing. Chill for 30 minutes, then transfer the salad to a lettuce-lined plate or glass bowl and top with the remaining whipped cream.

CABBAGE ROLL PIE

KAPUSTNY RULET

◆ ◆ ◆

This recipe gives stuffed cabbage rolls, that favourite East European dish, a distinct Estonian-Finnish twist, by burying the rolls under a layer of puffy yeast dough.

SERVES 6–8

- ◆ *100 g/4 oz pearl barley*
- ◆ *1.5 kg/3 lb head white Dutch cabbage*
- ◆ *30 ml/2 tbsp vegetable oil*
- ◆ *1 onion, finely chopped*
- ◆ *1 small red sweet pepper, cored, seeded and chopped*
- ◆ *225 g/8 oz minced lean pork*
- ◆ *225 g/8 oz minced veal*
- ◆ *2 sweet-sour dill gherkins, chopped*
- ◆ *275 ml/10 fl oz chicken or beef stock*
- ◆ *salt and freshly ground black pepper*
- ◆ *25 g/1 oz butter*
- ◆ *4 tsp flour*
- ◆ *15 ml/1 tbsp tomato purée*
- ◆ *150 ml/¹/₄ pt sour cream*
- ◆ *¹/₂ recipe sour-cream rye dough (page 77) or 450 g/1 lb packet wholewheat bread dough*
- ◆ *1 large egg*

Fill a large saucepan with water. Bring to the boil, add the barley and lower the heat. Simmer, covered, until the barley is tender, about 30 minutes. Drain the barley thoroughly and reserve.

Meanwhile, soften and remove the cabbage leaves as described on page 45. Repeat the process until you have about 18 leaves. Cut out the toughest part of the central stem in each leaf. Set aside.

Heat the oil in a frying pan and stir in the onion. Sauté until limp, about 6 minutes. Add the pepper and cook for another 5 minutes, until that too is limp. Take the mixture off the heat. Transfer to a bowl and add the meat, chopped gherkins, 30 ml/2 tbsp stock and salt and pepper to taste. Use your hands to combine well and divide into as many portions as there are leaves. Put a portion at the stalk end of each leaf, tuck in the ends, and roll to make a neat packet. Place the cabbage rolls in a baking dish just large enough to hold them in one layer. Set aside.

Melt the butter in a saucepan. Stir in the flour and cook for 3 minutes, or until the mixture is smooth. Whisk in the remaining stock and tomato purée; continue until the sauce boils and thickens. Take the sauce off the heat and stir in the sour cream. Pour the hot sauce evenly over the cabbage rolls.

Roll the dough out to a rectangle just larger than the baking dish. Lay over the top of the cabbage rolls and tuck the edges in. Use a fork to pull the dough gently towards the rim of the dish, crimping it. Cover the pastry with a dampened tea towel and leave to rise in a warm place for 20 minutes, or until risen and puffed up.

Preheat the oven to 180°C/350°F/Gas Mark 4. Make an egg wash by lightly beating the egg with a little water. Brush the wash over the pastry and bake until golden brown, about 45 minutes.

PORK LOIN WITH APPLE PRESERVES

SVINOYE FILYE Z KONSERVIROVANNYMI YABLOKAMI

◆ ◆ ◆

The accompanying preserve for this dish must be made at least 3 days ahead of time; the meat should be marinated for 24 hours. Leftover cooked meat, topped with the apple chutney, makes a particularly good cold sandwich on rye bread.

SERVES 4

- ◆ *1 kg/2lb rolled pork loin*
- ◆ *100 ml/4 fl oz lager*

For the marinade

- ◆ *15 ml/1 tbsp honey*
- ◆ *1 tbsp finely chopped fresh marjoram*
- ◆ *1 tsp juniper berries, crushed*
- ◆ *1 clove garlic, crushed*
- ◆ *¹/₄ tsp dried black peppercorns*

For the preserve

- ◆ *75 ml/3 fl oz dry apple cider*
- ◆ *175 g/6 oz light brown sugar*
- ◆ *3 dessert apples, peeled, cored and chopped*
- ◆ *1 small onion, finely chopped*
- ◆ *juice and rind of ¹/₂ lemon*
- ◆ *¹/₂ red sweet pepper, cored, seeded and chopped*
- ◆ *1 clove garlic, crushed and finely chopped*
- ◆ *2 tbsp finely chopped fresh peeled ginger*
- ◆ *large pinch cayenne pepper*
- ◆ *¹/₄ tsp salt*

Make the preserve first. Bring the cider and brown sugar to the boil in a large saucepan; stir until the sugar dissolves. Add the remaining ingredients and bring to the boil again. Reduce the heat and simmer, stirring occasionally, until the mixture is reduced to about 425 ml/³/₄ pt. Cool, then chill for at least 3 days before using. (The preserve may be kept for up to 2 weeks in the refrigerator.)

Place the marinade ingredients in a large plastic bag. Add the pork loin and roll it around in the bag to coat it. Tie the bag shut and place on a dish in a cool place. Turn it occasionally in the next 24 hours.

Preheat the oven to 190°C/375°F/Gas Mark 5. Decant the pork from the marinade and discard the marinade. Place the pork on a trivet over a baking tray and roast until the meat is done, about 50-55 minutes. Remove the meat to a dish and keep warm.

Skim the fat from the drippings in the tray and discard. Pour the lager into the tray and bring the boil over high heat, stirring the dripping into the lager. Reduce the liquid until thickened. Pour into a sauceboat and serve with the pork and preserves.

Pork Loin with Apple Preserves

POULTRY & MEAT

PICKLED AND COOKED GOOSE

GUS PRIGOTOVLYENNY V MARINADYE

◆ ◆ ◆

The cooking of Eastern Scandinavia has had a pronounced influence on the cuisine of Estonia. This recipe is a variation of an old Swedish dish; like ham, the cured bird could be kept until needed, a boon when refrigerators were unknown. The berry condiment is a typical Estonian touch.

SERVES 8

◆ *juice of ¹/₂ lemon*
◆ *225 g/8 oz salt*
◆ *1¹/₂ tsp saltpetre*
◆ *4.5 kg/10 lb goose, cleaned washed and dried*

◆ *225 g/8 oz canned lingonberries or cran- berries, crushed*

For the brine and poaching broth

◆ *50 g/2 oz salt and 15 g/¹/₂ oz sugar to each 600 ml/1 pt water*
◆ *1 medium onion, unpeeled*

◆ *1 carrot, scraped*
◆ *1 clove garlic, unpeeled*
◆ *6 whole black peppercorns*
◆ *2 bay leaves*

Combine the lemon juice, salt, sugar and saltpetre in a bowl. Rub the goose all over inside and out with the mixture, being sure to reach all parts. Place in a shallow non-metal baking dish or pan and set aside in a cool place for 24 hours, turning it several times.

Place the goose in a large saucepan or pot. Add enough water to cover it and more, with about 4 cm/1¹/₂ in to spare. Remove the goose and transfer the water with a measuring cup to a large bowl. Pour the water back into the pot and add salt and sugar in the proportions given in the ingredients above. Bring the brine to a rolling boil over high heat, then remove from the heat and leave to cool to room temperature.

When the brine is cool, put the goose into it. Weight the goose down to make sure it is totally submerged (a small weight inside the goose or a plate on top will do). Leave the bird in a cool place for 3 days, turning occasionally.

Lift out the goose and drain it thoroughly. Sew or skewer the openings shut and truss it. Place in a large saucepan or pot and add just enough water to cover. Drop in the vegetables, garlic, peppercorns and bay leaves and bring to the boil. Cover, lower the heat and simmer gently for about 1³/₄ hours or until the bird is fork-tender.

Drain the goose thoroughly and remove the trussing string and skewers. Serve warm or cold, with a sauceboat of the crushed lingonberries or cranberries on the side.

PASTRIES

SWEET CARAWAY BISCUITS

CEPUMI

◆ ◆ ◆

These sweet biscuits exhibit the Latvian love of caraway, even in sweet things.

MAKES ABOUT 48

◆ *100 g/4 oz unsalted butter, softened*
◆ *225 g/8 oz sugar*
◆ *1 egg*
◆ *2 tsp caraway seeds*

◆ *juice and grated rind of 1 small orange*
◆ *300 g/11 oz plain flour*
◆ *¹/₂ tsp baking soda*
◆ *¹/₄ tsp salt*

In a bowl, cream the butter with the sugar until light yellow and fluffy. Stir in the egg, caraway seeds, orange rind and 30ml/2 tbsp of the juice. Combine thoroughly.

Sift the flour and salt into a bowl and slowly stir into the butter mixture until you have a cohesive dough. Remove the dough from the bowl and place on a 300 cm/12 in long piece of greaseproof paper. Form the dough into a rough sausage and roll back and forth, wrapped in the paper, until the sausage is smooth and has become about 25 cm /10 in long and 5 cm/2 in wide. Wrap well in the paper and foil and freeze until solid. Preheat the oven to 180°C/350°F/Gas Mark 4. Cut the sausage into 1.5 cm/¹/₄ in slices and bake for 10–12 minutes, until the edges are golden brown.

Sweet Caraway Biscuits

SWEET APPLE BREAD PUDDING WITH LEMON SAUCE

SLADKY PUDDING Z YABLOKAMI I LIMONNOY PODLIVKOY

◆ ◆ ◆

The valued apple makes another appearance in this Lithuanian dessert, the sugar addict's answer to the savoury Potato and Apple Pudding on page 60. Vanilla ice cream makes a yummy cold partner for this warm pudding, as do mashed and sugared cranberries.

SERVES 6–8

- ◆ *100 g/4 oz unsalted butter*
- ◆ *400 ml/14 fl oz milk*
- ◆ *100 g/4 oz light brown sugar*
- ◆ *6 slices stale white bread, crusts removed, cubed*
- ◆ *2 dessert apples, peeled, cored and sliced*
- ◆ *2 eggs*
- ◆ *50 ml/2 fl oz Greek- or Bulgarian-style yoghurt*
- ◆ *¹/₂ tsp vanilla essence*
- ◆ *dash of almond essence*
- ◆ *¹/₄ tsp ground allspice*
- ◆ *¹/₄ tsp salt*
- ◆ *75 g/3 oz dates, stoned and finely chopped*
- ◆ *5 tsp wheatgerm*

For the sauce

- ◆ *175 g/6 oz sugar*
- ◆ *2 tbsp cornflour*
- ◆ *300 ml/¹/₂ pt water*
- ◆ *45 g/1¹/₂ oz butter*
- ◆ *45 ml/3 tbsp fresh lemon juice*

Heat the butter, milk and sugar together in a saucepan over low heat until the butter has melted and the sugar has dissolved. Set aside.

Combine the bread cubes and apple slices in a baking pan that will take them in one layer. In a bowl, whisk together the eggs, yoghurt, vanilla and almond essences, the allspice and salt. Stir in the milk mixture and the dates.

Pour the liquid over the apples and bread and leave to soak for 10–15 minutes. Meanwhile, preheat the oven to 180°C/350°F/Gas Mark 4. Sprinkle the top of the pudding with the wheatgerm and bake for 40 minutes, or until puffy and golden brown.

Meanwhile, make the sauce. In a saucepan, stir the sugar and cornflour in the water over high heat until boiling. Add the butter and lemon juice, stirring, and when the butter is dissolved, remove from the heat.

Serve the apple bread pudding warm, accompanied by the warm lemon sauce.

BERRY DESSERT PANCAKES

PANNKOOGID

◆ ◆ ◆

These Estonian pancakes are huge – the size of plates – and have a fluffy consistency quite unlike the familiar pancake. In their native surroundings they would often be served with lingonberries – but raspberries or blueberries are just as scrumptious.

SERVES 6

- ◆ *100 g/4 oz plain flour*
- ◆ *25 g/1 oz sugar*
- ◆ *pinch of salt*
- ◆ *2 eggs, separated*
- ◆ *225 ml/8 fl oz milk*
- ◆ *¹/₂ tsp vanilla essence*

For the filling

- ◆ *225/ 8 oz fresh raspberries or blueberries*
- ◆ *30 ml/2 tbsp water*
- ◆ *100 g/4 oz sugar*
- ◆ *1 tbsp cornflour*

Sift the flour, sugar and salt into a large bowl. Make a well in the centre. Drop the egg yolks, the milk and vanilla into the well, then beat to combine thoroughly with the flour. The batter will be thin. Cover it with a cloth and leave in a cool – not cold – place overnight to mature.

To make the filling, rinse and drain the berries and place in an enamelled or stainless steel saucepan, together with the water and the sugar. Cook over medium-high heat, stirring, until the berries are dissolving into a sauce, with some remaining whole. Bring to the boil, stir in the cornflour and reduce the heat. Cook for 5–10 minutes, stirring until the filling mixture has thickened. Remove from the heat, pour into an attractive bowl and allow to cool.

Before using the batter, beat the egg whites in a large bowl until they form stiff peaks. With a rubber or plastic spatula, carefully fold them into the batter.

Lightly coat a large non-stick crêpe or frying pan with butter and heat until medium-hot. Remove from the heat and pour in 100 ml/4 fl oz of the batter. Tilt the pan to spread it evenly, then replace on the heat and fry the pancake for about 3 minutes a side, until golden. Slide the pancake on to a dish and keep warm while you make the rest of the pancakes.

Serve each pancake flat on a plate, accompanied by the bowl of fruit sauce.

4

FROM FARMLAND AND BREADBASKET

Ukraine, Belorussia and Moldova

ALL THREE EASTERN STATES OF THE CIS SHARE
A COMMON LEGACY OF 'BORDERDOM', BUT EACH HAS
RESPONDED TO ITS SITUATION IN A DIFFERENT WAY.
BELORUSSIA AND MOLDOVA EXHIBIT PERHAPS STRONGER
CHARACTERISTICS OF THEIR GENEALOGICAL 'DISTAFF'
SIDES – POLAND AND ROMANIA RESPECTIVELY –
BUT THEY HAVE SHOWN THEMSELVES LESS VOLATILE
POLITICALLY AND LESS NATIONALISTIC THAN
THE UKRAINIAN GIANT.

Though a separate republic with a people fiercely proud of their different language, literature, culture and cuisine, the Ukraine is, in fact, the cradle of Russian civilization. Kiev, its capital, was originally the premier town and capital of Russ, the first unified 'Russian-Slavic' state, founded in the 9th century. At its height, the kingdom stretched from the Baltic to the Volga and Danube; its rulers crushed invaders from the south and east and assimilated its previous Scandinavian lords. However, by the 12th and 13th centuries disputes over successions, devastating attacks by the Tartars and the expansion of the Polish-Lithuanian alliance had pushed the centre of power to the east – to Novgorod and eventually to Moscow.

The early importance of Kiev-Rus is echoed in the influence of Ukrainian food. The ubiquitous beetroot was an introduction to Russia from the Ukraine, as was *borsch* itself. Here even the green tops of the beet are treated with respect. Peter the Great's present to his people, the potato, was exploited to the fullest in the fields and kitchens of the Ukraine and Belorussia, to make its circuitous way back into the repertoire of heartland Russia. There is good reason too why the Ukraine was known as the 'breadbasket' of the old Union; both fields of grain and traditional creativity in baking have resulted in a fabled 70 types of loaves, rolls and buns, ranging from white to black, plain or studded with caraway or poppy seeds, and flavoured with rye, sour cream, honey or molasses.

Within the old Soviet Union, the Ukrainians have always carried a reputation as chefs, using a greater variety both of ingredients and cooking methods than the Russians. Because the Ukraine stretches into the Crimea, historical home to immigrant Tartars and Turks as well as Slavs, eastern influences permeated northwards. From these regions came the Eastern and Middle-Eastern taste for honey, nuts, citrus and dried fruits in both sweet and savoury dishes.

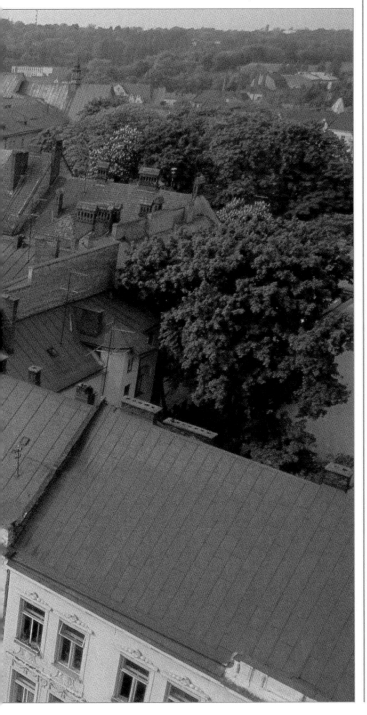

The cooking of the small republics of Belorussia and Moldova exhibit notably more 'non-Russian' tendencies than that of their huge sprawling neighbour to the north. The borders of the former have moved east and west between Russia and Poland for centuries, and the food of the region displays that dichotomy. Pigs have overtaken cattle in agricultural and culinary importance, while Eastern Polish specialities like pork crackling in dripping (used as a spread for bread), a wide variety of ham sausages, *zrazy* (beef rolls stuffed with sour pickles, eggs and/or vegetables), Polish-style *golubtsy* (without tomatoes or sour cream), the preference of sauerkraut to fresh cabbage and a weakness for poppyseed pastries became Belorussian fixtures. As in urban Poland, the cuisines of Minsk and Brest show the influence of the huge Jewish communities which once flourished there.

Moldova, to all intents and purposes, is an outpost of Romania. Its stews and sausages can be surprisingly spicy; red and haricot beans, sweetcorn, fresh peppers, grilled meats and fresh, smoked and aged ewe's cheeses speak more of the Balkans and the Levant than of northern steppes. Here too begins the wine belt that extends into the Crimea and on to Georgia; its vineyards boast more than 100 varieties of red, white, rosé and champagne wines. Unfamiliar with modern technological developments in oenology, their labels unknown in the west, they promise a bonanza for future generations of wine lovers once the new openness in communications allows progress to make its way in this time-locked region.

◁ *Lvov, in the Ukraine, was the scene of violent nationalist demonstrations in October 1989. In more peaceful times, the gilded,* **fin-de-siècle** *opera theatre* (centre) *is a focus for the city's cultural activity.*

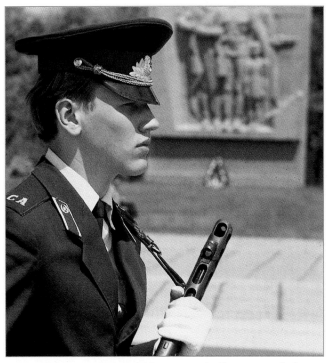

In Kishinev, capital of Moldova, a guard of honour patrols the monument to soldiers killed in the Second World War.

'ALMOST NOTHING' SOUP

POCHTY NICHEVO

◆ ◆ ◆

This soup, made from scraps, has a surprising flavour, smoky and nut-like. Add a little cream to make it more sophisticated.

SERVES 4 – 6

- ◆ *1.5 kg/3 lb beef, chicken, veal or mixed bones*
- ◆ *1 onion, unpeeled*
- ◆ *salt and freshly ground black pepper*
- ◆ *1.75 litres/3¹/₄ pt water*
- ◆ *1 kg/2 lb potatoes, scrubbed and dried*
- ◆ *100ml/4oz bacon fat or melted butter*
- ◆ *100 ml/4 fl oz single cream (optional)*
- ◆ *2 tbsp chopped fresh chives*

Place the bones, the unpeeled onion and seasoning to taste in a large pot. Cover with the water and put over high heat. Bring to the boil, then cover and simmer for 1 hour. Uncover and continue to simmer until the stock has reduced to almost half. Strain the stock and return to the saucepan.

Meanwhile peel the potatoes. Reserve the potatoes themselves for another use. Melt the bacon fat or butter in a frying pan and sauté the onion until soft, about 6 minutes. Add the potato skins and continue to cook until they too are tender.

Transfer the potato skins and onion to the saucepan containing the stock. Bring to the boil, then reduce the heat and simmer for 10 minutes. Purée the soup in batches; return to the saucepan and reheat. Thin, if necessary, with a little water or the single cream. Ladle into individual bowls and serve sprinkled with the chopped chives.

BLACK BREAD SOUP

ZUPA KHLEBOVA

◆ ◆ ◆

This is another soup born of poverty and bad harvests –
yet it is filling and extremely flavourful. It is a meal in itself
rather than a delicate preliminary to an elegant repast
and can be accompanied by warm *pierogi* and followed by
salad. Ukrainian croutons are traditionally fried in pork
dripping or bacon fat.

SERVES 6

- 1 large carrot, halved and sliced
- 1 large leek, sliced
- 1 celery stick, sliced
- 2 onions, chopped
- 1 parsnip, chopped
- 100 g/4 oz broad beans
- 1.25 litres/2¹/₄ pt beef stock
- 175 g/6 oz stale black bread, cubed
- salt and freshly ground black pepper
- 150 ml/¹/₄ pt buttermilk
- 100 ml/4 fl oz milk
- 2 large egg yolks, lightly beaten
- fried croutons
- large pinch of nutmeg

Place all the vegetables in a large saucepan. Add the beef stock
and bring to a boil over high heat. Add the bread, reduce the
heat, cover and simmer for about 40 minutes or until all the
vegetables are tender.

Purée the soup in batches in a blender or food processor
until as smooth as possible; return to the saucepan. Add
seasoning to taste and stir in the buttermilk and milk. Heat
until simmering, but do not boil.

Spoon a small amount of the hot soup into the beaten eggs,
then quickly stir the eggs into the soup in the saucepan.
Remove from the heat immediately and pour the soup into a
tureen. Scatter fried croutons over the top and a sprinkling of
nutmeg; offer more croutons in a separate bowl.

MOLDOVAN POTATO-CHEESE SOUP

MOLDAVSKY SUP IZ SYRA I KARTOPHELYA

◆ ◆ ◆

This is a soup for potato-lovers, traditionally made with
aged *brynza*, a hard ewe's cheese. It is lip-smacking good
made with the Basque variety. You can use Cheddar instead
of ewe's cheese, but the results will not be as authentic.

SERVES 6

- 50 g/2 oz unsalted butter
- 2 large onions, finely chopped
- 3 large carrots, chopped
- 2 large potatoes, peeled and chopped
- ¹/₄ tsp sweet paprika
- large pinch of cayenne pepper
- 1 tbsp finely chopped parsley
- 1.25 litres/2 pt chicken stock
- 225 g/8 oz ewe's cheese (Basque Ektori or similar) or Cheddar
- salt and freshly ground black pepper
- finely snipped chives

Melt the butter in a large saucepan over medium heat.
Add the onions and carrots and sauté gently for about 20–25
minutes, until they are tender and lightly coloured.

Stir in the potatoes, spices and parsley, then add the
chicken stock and bring to the boil. Reduce the heat, cover,
and simmer for 30 minutes, or until the potatoes are soft.

Strain the soup into a bowl and purée the vegetables in a
blender or food processor with a little of the stock until
smooth. Return the purée to the saucepan and add as much
stock as necessary (about 1 litre/1³/₄ pt) to obtain a good
consistency. Set the soup over low heat and stir in the cheese.

Continue stirring until it has dissolved into the soup, but do
not allow to boil. Adjust the seasoning to taste and serve
immediately in individual bowls, topped with the snipped
chives.

BREADS

GRILLED CORNMEAL CAKE WITH CHEESE
MAMALYGA
◆ ◆ ◆

Moldovan food exhibits a legacy of the days between the wars when it was a part of Romania, and of the generations before that when it had many unofficial links with that country. This polenta-like hard cake has a Balkan flavour; it is often served with *borsch* or cabbage dishes.

SERVES 6

◆ *150 g/5 oz stone-ground yellow cornmeal*
◆ *1 litre/1³/₄ pt water*
◆ *1–1¹/₂ tsp salt*
◆ *50 g/2 oz butter*
◆ *pinch of dried marjoram*

◆ *large pinch of cayenne pepper*
◆ *275 g/10 oz hard ewe's or goat's cheese, or Lancashire cheese*
◆ *salt and freshly ground black pepper*

Stir the cornmeal in a large frying pan over medium heat for 4 minutes, or until it loses its bright yellow colour and becomes light beige.

Pour the water into a saucepan. Put the hot cornmeal into the water, it should hiss; then stir in the salt to taste. Cook over moderate heat for 5 minutes, stirring, until the liquid begins to boil. Cover, lower the heat and simmer for 20 minutes, stirring frequently.

Preheat the oven to 190°C/375°F/Gas Mark 5. Uncover the saucepan and continue to stir until the polenta is very thick and the spoon is drawing it away from the bottom and sides of the pan. Remove from the heat, add the butter, marjoram and pepper, and stir until the butter is melted into the polenta. Stir in three-quarters of the cheese, then turn the polenta into a shallow buttered baking dish.

Bake for 40 minutes on the top shelf of the oven, until the cake has a skin over it. Remove from the oven and allow to cool and set for at least 1 hour. (The cake can be kept refrigerated for up to 3 days.)

To serve, heat the grill to hot. Slice the cake into squares or wedges and sprinkle over the remaining cheese. Grill until the cheesy crust is golden-brown and the *mamalyga* is hot. Serve immediately.

SOUR CREAM RYE ROLLS

BALABUSKY

◆ ◆ ◆

The Ukraine is renowned for the variety of its breads. These rolls are one of the types most commonly encountered. They make delicious sandwiches when filled with smoked ham, kolbasa or salt beef, spread with plenty of mustard.

MAKES 10–12 ROLLS

◆ *175 ml/6 fl oz lukewarm water*
◆ *2½ tsp (1 x 8g/¼ oz packet) active dry yeast*
◆ *1 tbsp sugar*
◆ *100 ml/4 fl oz sour cream*
◆ *100 g/4 oz rye flour*
◆ *225–275 g/8–10 oz plain flour*
◆ *1½–2 tsp salt*
◆ *1½ tbsp caraway seeds*

Place the water in a large bowl and sprinkle the yeast and sugar into it. Leave for 5–8 minutes, or until the mixture is foamy. Stir in the sour cream, then slowly work in the rye flour and 225 g/8 oz of the plain flour. Add salt to taste and 1 tbsp of the caraway seeds. Work the dough with your hands until it forms a ball and turn out on to a floured surface. Knead in as much of the remaining flour as will make the dough smooth and still slightly sticky; this will take about 8–10 minutes.

Transfer the dough to a buttered bowl, turning it to coat with butter, then cover the bowl with cling film and leave to rise in a warm place for 1 hour or until doubled in volume. Turn the dough out on to a floured surface and pull into 10–12 equal pieces. Shape each into a flat-bottomed oval, scatter the remaining caraway seeds over the tops and press in lightly.

Place the ovals on a lightly-oiled baking tray and leave to rise, covered with a damp tea towel, for 45–60 minutes, or until doubled in size.

Preheat the oven to 200°C/400°F/Gas Mark 6. Bake the rolls for 18–20 minutes, or until they are golden brown. (The rolls may be frozen. Reheat wrapped in foil for 30 minutes at 190°C/375°F/Gas Mark 5.)

EGG NOODLES AND BUCKWHEAT GROATS

LOKSHYNA Z KASHA

◆ ◆ ◆

Noodles and dumplings of all types are popular in the Ukraine and Belorussia. They range from little misshapen egg pasta droplets to potato and rice dumplings. They are served on their own with butter, accompanied by meat sauces, or baked with other ingredients, as here.

SERVES 6–8

◆ *100 g/4 oz unsalted butter*
◆ *2 onions, sliced*
◆ *225 g/8 oz field or brown mushrooms, sliced*
◆ *175 g/6 oz whole buckwheat groats (kasha)*
◆ *1 large egg, beaten*
◆ *425 ml/³/₄ pt boiling water*
◆ *1 tsp salt*
◆ *225 g/8 oz fresh egg noodles, cut into quarters*
◆ *freshly ground black pepper*
◆ *50 g/2 oz fine dry breadcrumbs*
◆ *sour cream*

Melt 25 g/1 oz butter in a large frying pan and sauté the onions until they are soft and lightly coloured, about 8 minutes. Add the mushrooms and cook, stirring, until the mushrooms are soft. Transfer the vegetables to a casserole.

Wash and dry the frying pan. Place over moderate heat and add the buckwheat, stirring, and the beaten egg. Continue to stir until the groats are separate and egg-coated. Pour in the boiling water and add 15 g/½ oz butter and the salt. Cover and simmer until all the liquid is absorbed and the buckwheat just tender, about 25 minutes. Transfer the buckwheat to the casserole.

Preheat the oven to 180°C/350°F/Gas Mark 4. In a large saucepan, cook the noodles in boiling water until just tender, about 4 minutes. Drain thoroughly and stir the noodles into the casserole with the buckwheat, onions and mushrooms, adding 45 g/1½ oz butter and seasoning to taste. Melt the remaining butter and combine with the breadcrumbs. Scatter over the top of the casserole and bake in the oven until warmed through and the breadcrumbs are toasted, about 20 minutes. Serve with a sauceboat of sour cream.

MINSK-STYLE EGGS

JAJKA MINSKY

◆ ◆ ◆

These eggs make a frequent appearance at Christmas and Easter festivities. They are traditionally eaten warm, with horn spoons, but they are also good cold.

SERVES 8

- *10 hard-boiled eggs*
- *75 g/3 oz unsalted butter, softened*
- *15 ml/1 tbsp mayonnaise*
- *30 ml/2 tbsp double cream*
- *3$\frac{1}{2}$ tbsp fresh dill*
- *2 tsp sweet paprika*
- *1 tbsp finely chopped fresh parsley*
- *4 tbsp dry breadcrumbs*
- *3 tbsp grated Gruyère cheese*
- *16 anchovy fillets, rinsed, dried and cut in half lengthways*
- *fresh watercress sprigs*

Halve the eggs and carefully remove the yolks. Set aside the 16 best whites.

In a bowl, mash the yolks well with the softened butter. Beat in the mayonnaise, double cream, dill, paprika, parsley and seasoning to taste. Finely chop the 4 extra whites and stir them into the mixture. Divide the filling between the 16 reserved egg whites.

Preheat the oven to 200°C/400°F/Gas Mark 6. Place the filled eggs on a baking tray. Mix together the breadcrumbs and grated cheese and sprinkle evenly over the yolks. Cross each egg with two strips of anchovy to make an 'X'. Bake for 10 minutes, until the eggs are warmed through and the tops are golden.

Arrange sprigs of watercress on 8 plates, and put 2 egg-halves on each plate. Serve warm.

ODESSA-STYLE MUSHROOMS IN SOUR CREAM

ZULYNEZ GRIBNOY PO-ODESSKY

◆ ◆ ◆

The combination of mushrooms and sour cream is a popular one all over the Ukraine, Belorussia and Moldova and understandably, as it is mouthwateringly delicious. However, the version that originates from the holiday port of Odessa, on the Black Sea, has a widespread reputation among cognoscenti. At home it would be made with *brynza* or *seerh*, but Lancashire or Caerphilly cheese make good substitutes.

SERVES 6

- *90 g/3$\frac{1}{2}$ oz unsalted butter, at room temperature*
- *4 spring onions, finely chopped*
- *450 g/1 lb field or brown mushrooms, wiped and patted dry*
- *1 tbsp flour*
- *salt and freshly ground black pepper*
- *100 ml/4 fl oz sour cream*
- *75 ml/3 fl oz double cream*
- *50 g/2 oz Lancashire or Caerphilly cheese, grated*

Melt 50 g/2 oz of the butter in a frying pan over medium heat. Add the spring onions and sauté briefly, then stir in the mushrooms and continue to cook for about 5–6 minutes, until the mushrooms are browned and just going soft.

In a small bowl, combine 15 g/$\frac{1}{2}$ oz butter with the flour, working it to make a *beurre manié*. Stir the *beurre manié* into the mushrooms and cook for 3 minutes, or until thickened. Season to taste, and stir in the sour cream and double cream.

Preheat the oven to 180°C/350°F/Gas Mark 4. Pour the mushroom mixture into an attractive baking dish. Sprinkle the top with the cheese, and dot with the remaining butter. Bake for 20–25 minutes, until the mushrooms are bubbling and the top just colouring.

Odessa Style Mushrooms in Sour Cream

PICKLED WATERMELON RIND

MARINOVANNYA ARBUZNAYA KORKA

◆ ◆ ◆

Pickled watermelon rind is a common addition to a *zakuska* table, its sweet-sour tang a perfect complement to meat- and cheese-based dishes.

MAKES ABOUT 1.75 LITRES/3 PT

- ◆ *1 kg/2 lb watermelon rind*
- ◆ *100 g/4 oz salt*
- ◆ *2.75 litres/4$^1/_2$ pt water*
- ◆ *600 ml/1 pt cider vinegar*
- ◆ *1 tsp whole cloves*
- ◆ *1 cinnamon stick*
- ◆ *2 slices root ginger, peeled and crushed*
- ◆ *1 tsp whole allspice*
- ◆ *1 kg/2 lb sugar*

Pare the rind carefully of any pink flesh and remove the thin green peel on the surface. Cut into 2.5 x 1 cm/1 x $^1/_2$ in pieces. Place them in a bowl with the salt and 2.25 litres/4 pt water to cover. Leave overnight.

Drain the rind, rinse thoroughly with cold water, and drain again. Put the rind in a large enamelled or stainless steel saucepan with 300 ml/$^1/_2$ pt water and the vinegar. Cover and boil the rind, stirring occasionally, until it is softened. Tie the spices in a muslin bag and drop into the pot; stir in the sugar until it is dissolved. Bring the mixture to the boil and cook over high heat until the rind is transparent.

Transfer the rind to sterilized Mason jars. Reduce the syrup a further 5 minutes, then pour over the rinds and seal the jars. Allow to cool, then keep in a cold dark place until needed.

CABBAGE SOUFFLÉ

NAKYPLIAK

◆ ◆ ◆

***Nakypliak* is considered the test of a good Ukrainian cook. Following traditional methods of preparation and steaming, it takes several days and much work to prepare, but this version cuts a few corners – it still requires time, but the workload has been lightened. The result is still a revelation.**

SERVES 4

- ◆ *$^1/_2$ a small white cabbage (about 375 g/12 oz), outer leaves removed, cored and cut into three wedges*
- ◆ *salt and freshly ground black pepper*
- ◆ *large pinch of sweet paprika*
- ◆ *$^1/_4$ tsp caraway seeds*
- ◆ *75 g/3 oz bacon fat or butter*
- ◆ *1 onion, finely chopped*
- ◆ *1 clove garlic, crushed*
- ◆ *3 tbsp flour*
- ◆ *large pinch of cayenne pepper*
- ◆ *200ml/7fl oz milk*
- ◆ *150 g/5 oz Gruyère cheese, grated*
- ◆ *3 eggs separated*
- ◆ *2 tbsp breadcrumbs mixed with a little melted butter*

Shred the cabbage wedges as thinly as possible and place in a large bowl with a wide mouth. Sprinkle 2 tsp salt over the cabbage. Toss, and squeeze the salt into the cabbage to soften it. Place a plate on top of the cabbage, and a small weight on the plate. Place a tea towel over the top of the bowl. Leave for several hours in a warm place (for example an airing cupboard), until the cabbage is juicy. Then pour boiling water over the cabbage so that the plate is just submerged and tie the tea towel over the bowl. Leave the bowl in a warm place for 3–4 days before continuing with the recipe.

When ready to proceed, drain the cabbage. Rinse it thoroughly in cold water, then drain well again. Place the cabbage in a saucepan, add a little boiling water and the caraway seeds, and cook over low heat, uncovered, for about 20 minutes, stirring occasionally until the cabbage is soft and the water evaporated. Drain the cabbage in a colander, pressing with a spoon to make sure that as much liquid as possible has been removed. Allow the cabbage to cool to room temperature.

Meanwhile, melt the bacon fat or butter in a flameproof casserole and sauté the onion until soft and lightly coloured, about 6 minutes. Add the garlic and cook for another 2 minutes, then stir in the flour and cook for a further 2 minutes. Take off the heat and stir in the cayenne pepper, paprika and seasoning to taste and, little by little, the milk. Return to the heat and bring to the boil, stirring until it begins to thicken. Remove from the heat again and beat in the cheese, followed by the egg yolks.

Preheat the oven to 190°C/375°F/Gas Mark 5. Stir the cooled cabbage into the sauce. In a bowl, whisk the egg whites until stiff but not dry. Fold them lightly into the cabbage mixture. Spoon the mixture into a greased soufflé dish and scatter the breadcrumbs over the top. Bake in the oven for 40 minutes until risen, lightly browned and set. Serve at once, piping hot.

Chicken Kiev

Kotlety po-Kievsky

◆ ◆ ◆

**Chicken Kiev has become a familiar dish, stacked frozen
and ready-to-heat in supermarkets and frequently
appearing on menus, even in pubs. But the real thing bears
little resemblance, in appearance or taste, to such orange
monstrosities. The recipe has been simplified to take
advantage of prepared chicken breasts.**

SERVES 6

- *150 g/6 oz unsalted butter, softened*
- *grated rind and juice of 1 large lemon*
- *3 tbsp freshly chopped tarragon*
- *6 large skinless chicken breast fillets*
- *salt and freshly ground black pepper*
- *2 small eggs*
- *175 g/6 oz fresh fine breadcrumbs*
- *oil for deep-frying*

Combine the butter, lemon rind and tarragon in a bowl. With a fork, work the mixture until it is thoroughly mixed. Shape into a block, wrap in foil, and chill until hard.

Lay the chicken breasts on a sheet of greaseproof paper. Trim away any bits attached by membrane. Cover the breasts with another sheet of greaseproof paper and pound with a mallet until they are flattened. Season the fillets as desired.

Cut the butter block into 6 pieces and place one piece in the centre of each fillet. Fold the top and edges over, then roll neatly. Tie the roll with thread.

Beat the eggs lightly in a shallow bowl. Spread the breadcrumbs on a large plate. Dip the breast rolls in the egg then coat them in the breadcrumbs, pressing into the crumbs to make sure they adhere. To obtain a thick 'skin' brush the coated rolls with a little more egg if necessary and press into the crumbs again. Place the rolls on a plate and chill for 2–3 hours.

In a deep fryer or heavy saucepan, heat enough oil to cover the breasts completely. When it spits at water droplets (or reaches 190°/375°F), lower in 3 breasts with a slotted spoon. Fry until golden-brown, about 5–6 minutes. (The oil must not get too hot or the coating will brown before the chicken is cooked.) Drain on absorbent kitchen paper and repeat with the remaining 3 breasts. Serve immediately. Potatoes and cabbage or peas would make a typical accompaniment.

STEWED LAMB WITH MUSHROOMS AND BARLEY

TYSHYONAYA BARANINAZ GRIBAMI I YACHMENYOM

◆ ◆ ◆

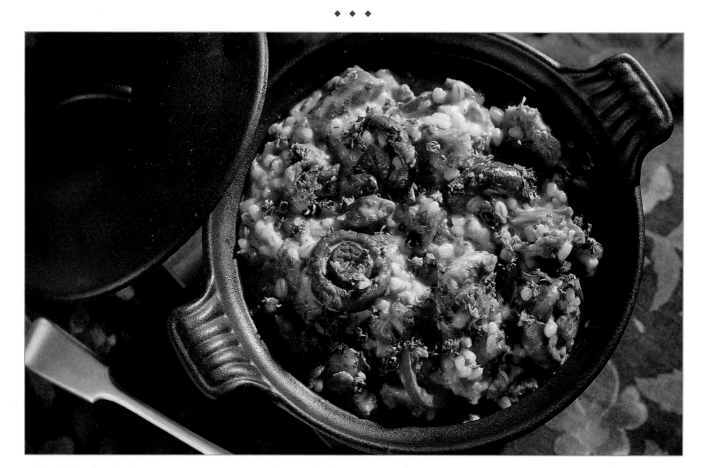

This is a Moldovan dish, from the foothills of the Carpathian mountains. It is unsophisticated and hardly pretty-pretty, but it is nutritious, inexpensive and full-flavoured, a true rustic feast.

SERVES 6

- 1.25 kg/2¹/₂ lb shanks or neck of lamb, cut into pieces
- 90 ml/ 3¹/₂ fl oz vegetable oil
- 1 medium onion, chopped
- 2 long red medium-hot peppers, seeded and chopped
- 175 g/6 oz field or button mushrooms, wiped and sliced
- 15 ml/1 tbsp German-style mustard
- 700 ml/1¹/₄ pt chicken stock
- 75 ml/3 fl oz white wine vinegar
- 225 g/8 oz pearl barley
- 1 tsp cumin seeds
- 2 whole cloves
- 2 tsp dried dill
- salt and freshly ground black pepper
- 225 ml/8 fl oz sour cream or yoghurt
- 50 g/2 oz flat-leaved parsley, finely chopped

In a heavy casserole, brown the lamb shank or neck pieces in half the oil until they are coloured. Remove with a slotted spoon and set aside. Add the onion to the casserole, and cook until it is soft and lightly coloured, about 6–8 minutes. Remove with the slotted spoon and set aside. Add the rest of the oil and sauté the red peppers and mushroom for about 5 minutes, or until the mushrooms are softened. Remove to a bowl and set aside.

Preheat the oven to 170°C/325°F/Gas Mark 3. Stir the onions and lamb back into the casserole, together with the mustard. Add the chicken stock and the wine vinegar, bring to the boil, and transfer the casserole to the oven. Bake for 1¹/₂ hours, until the lamb is very tender and falling off the bones.

Remove the lamb from the casserole. Using your hands and a fork, pull the meat from the bones and chop it. Return to the casserole and stir into the stock with the barley, cumin seeds, cloves, dill and seasoning to taste. Bring to the boil, cover and lower the heat. Simmer for about 1 hour, until the barley is tender and most of the stock has been absorbed.

Stir the red pepper and mushrooms into the stew, together with the sour cream or yoghurt. Heat through for about 10–12 minutes, take off the heat, stir in the chopped parsley, and bring to the table to serve.

SPICED OXTAILS WITH BUCKWHEAT

BYCHYI KHVOSTY Z KASHEY

◆ ◆ ◆

In the Russian and Polish countryside you can still see oxen pulling ploughs and rough-looking horses trotting in front of wooden carts. A tough, gelatinous meat, oxtail needs slow cooking but the resulting tender flesh, falling off the bone, and the rich, thick sauce are worth the wait. This recipe is an adaptation from the Lower Volga region, nearing the Caspian Sea.

SERVES 6–8

- *2.25 kg/ 5 lb oxtail pieces, trimmed*
- *75 ml/3 fl oz sunflower oil*
- *3 medium onions, sliced*
- *4 cloves garlic, crushed*
- *23 ml/1 1/2 tbsp tomato purée*
- *400 ml/14 oz can chopped chilli tomatoes*
- *825 ml/1 1/2 pt beef stock*
- *3 cinnamon sticks*
- *1 tsp ground cumin*
- *1 tsp ground ginger*
- *1 tsp mustard seeds*
- *3/4 tsp turmeric*
- *4 tbsp finely chopped parsley*
- *4 tbsp finely chopped coriander*
- *350 g/12 oz coarse buckwheat groats*
- *600 ml/1 pt boiling water*
- *salt and freshly ground black pepper*
- *25 g/1 oz butter*
- *3 carrots, halved and thinly sliced*
- *375 g/12 oz turnips, halved and thinly sliced*
- *1 small celeriac, quartered and thinly sliced*
- *2 medium courgettes, halved and thinly sliced*
- *225 g/8 oz baby leeks, trimmed and left whole*
- *parsley and/or coriander sprigs, to garnish*

In a large enamelled or stainless steel casserole, brown the oxtails in the oil. Remove with a slotted spoon to a plate and set aside. Add the onion to the pot and fry gently over medium heat until lightly coloured and soft. Stir in the garlic and cook for 1 minute, then stir in the tomato purée, the tomatoes and their juice, and the beef stock. Drop in the cinnamon sticks, and stir in the cumin, ginger, mustard seeds, turmeric, parsley and coriander. Bring to the boil, then cover and lower the heat. Simmer for 4 hours over a low heat, until the meat from the larger pieces is falling off the bone. If necessary, add water to keep the stock covering the meat.

Take the casserole off the heat and allow to cool. Refrigerate for 12 hours or overnight .

Preheat the oven to 180°C/350°F/Gas Mark 4. Dry roast the buckwheat in a frying pan over medium-high heat, stirring constantly, until it begins to pop. Add the boiling water and salt to taste. Dot the butter over the surface and bake in the oven for 45 minutes, or until the grains are soft. Keep warm.

Meanwhile, lift off the solidified fat from the top of the casserole. With a slotted spoon, take out the oxtails, place them in a large baking dish and pour over enough boiling water to cover the bottom of the dish to about 1 cm/1/2 in. Cover the dish with foil and reheat in the oven for the last 30 minutes while the buckwheat is cooking.

Strain the stock from the casserole into a bowl and discard the solids. Return the stock to the casserole and add the carrots, turnips and celeriac. Bring to the boil, then cover and simmer the vegetables for 15 minutes, or until they are tender-crisp. Stir in the courgette slices and the baby leeks and cook for a further 5–10 minutes until they are also soft.

Drain the sauce through a strainer into a saucepan. Set the vegetables aside. Strain the reheated oxtails, allowing the cooking liquid to flow into the same saucepan. Quickly bring the sauce to a boil.

Pile the cooked buckwheat on to a large serving dish. Spoon the strained vegetables on top of the buckwheat and surround it with the oxtails. Drizzle some of the sauce over the vegetables and buckwheat and serve the remainder separately in a sauceboat. Garnish the dish with the sprigs of parsley and/or coriander.

NEMAN RIVER CARP IN KVAS AND LEMON

NEMANSKY KARP V KVASYE

◆ ◆ ◆

Though a staple of the Western Russian, Polish and Jewish diet, carp has not found much favour on the British table, largely because its bones make it a difficult fish to eat. This dish overcomes the problem, however, by boning the carp and cutting it into strips.

SERVES 6

- ◆ *1.75–2.25 kg/4–5 lb carp, cleaned, head and backbone removed*
- ◆ *salt and freshly ground black pepper*
- ◆ *45 g/1½ oz unsalted butter*
- ◆ *8 spring onions, finely chopped*
- ◆ *2 tsp brown sugar*
- ◆ *½ bay leaf*
- ◆ *5 juniper berries, crushed*
- ◆ *grated rind and juice of 1 small lemon*
- ◆ *425 ml/¾ pt kvas or flat beer*
- ◆ *3 tbsp crushed ginger biscuits*
- ◆ *50 g/2 oz flat-leaved parsley, finely chopped*

Wash and dry the fish thoroughly. Cut into 4 cm/1½ in wide strips and sprinkle with salt. Chill for 1 hour.

In a heavy enamelled or stainless-steel casserole, melt the butter over medium heat and sauté the onions for 2 minutes, stirring. Add the sugar, herbs, lemon juice and rind, and pepper to taste. Stir for a couple of minutes to combine then pour in the *kvas* and simmer for 20 minutes.

Strain into a bowl, discard the solids, then return the stock to the saucepan. Stir in the crushed ginger biscuits, and cook until they have dissolved into a mush. Add the fish, spoon the sauce over it, cover the casserole and cook over medium-low heat for about 12 minutes, or until the fish is opaque and just flaking.

Transfer the fish strips to a dish with a spatula and turn the heat to high to reduce the sauce slightly. Stir in the parsley and pour the sauce over the fish. Serve immediately.

POTATO DUMPLINGS WITH PRUNE AND NUT FILLING

KARTOPHELNYE VARENIKY

◆ ◆ ◆

Potatoes have a revered place in the East European kitchen, and are exploited fully. These dumplings are a speciality of the lower Ukraine and Moldova.

MAKES 32–36

- ◆ *800 g/1¾ lb floury potatoes, cooked, peeled, mashed and cooled*
- ◆ *200–224 g/7–8 oz plain flour*
- ◆ *75 g/3 oz lard*
- ◆ *1 egg yolk*
- ◆ *salt*
- ◆ *¼ tsp cinnamon*
- ◆ *50 g/2 oz fresh breadcrumbs, toasted*
- ◆ *100 g/4 oz sugar*

For the filling

- ◆ *15 ready-to-eat prunes*
- ◆ *½ tsp grated lemon rind*
- ◆ *15 ml/1 tbsp lemon juice*
- ◆ *45 g/1½ oz walnuts, finely chopped*
- ◆ *50 g/2 oz sugar*

Make the filling first. In a saucepan, just submerge the prunes in water. Bring to the boil, then lower the heat and simmer for 20 minutes. Cool the prunes in the liquid then drain them, reserving 30 ml/2 tbsp of the liquid. Stone and chop the prunes, place in a bowl and mix together with the lemon rind and juice, walnuts and sugar.

In a large bowl, beat the potatoes with 200 g/7 oz of the flour, the lard, egg yolk and salt to taste. Use your hands to work the mixture into a dough. Transfer to a floured surface and knead, adding a little more flour if necessary to get a smooth, glossy dough. Roll out until it is a large rectangle 7 mm/⅓ in thick, then cut into squares of about 8 cm/3½ in.

Place a heaped teaspoon of the filling in the centre of each square. Pull up the corners to enclose the filling and form the dough around it to make a ball.

Bring a large saucepan of salted water to the boil, drop in the dumplings and poach for about 25 minutes, or until they are glossy and float to the surface.

Drain the dumplings thoroughly. Mix together the cinnamon, breadcrumbs and sugar and roll the warm dumplings in the mixture. Serve immediately with soured cream.

Potato Dumplings with Prune and Nut Filling

ORANGES WITH SPICED RUM

APYELSINY V ROMYE Z PRYANOSTYAMI

◆ ◆ ◆

**While vodka is the most common strong spirit of
the people, *rhum* has always been used in cooking.**

SERVES 6

- ◆ *100 g/4 oz sugar*
- ◆ *2 tsp whole cloves*
- ◆ *350 ml/12 fl oz water*
- ◆ *30 ml/2 tbsp dark rum*
- ◆ *4–5 oranges, peeled, pith removed and sliced*

In a large saucepan, bring the sugar, cloves and water to the
boil. Continue to cook at medium-high heat until reduced by
a quarter, and quite syrupy. Remove from the heat and stir in
the rum. Leave to cool.

Place the sliced fruit in 6 individual glass bowls and pour
over the rum syrup. Chill for a couple of hours before serving.

SPICED HONEY CAKE

MEDIVNYK

◆ ◆ ◆

**This delicious cake should be made at least 3 days ahead to
let the flavours mature. It is a traditional part of Christmas
festivities – celebrated with more ceremony in Catholic parts
of the Ukraine and Belorussia than in Orthodox Russia,
though honey cake is very popular there too.**

SERVES 12

- ◆ *225 ml/8 fl oz plus 15 ml/1 tbsp dark honey*
- ◆ *1 tsp cinnamon*
- ◆ *1/2 tsp ground nutmeg*
- ◆ *1/2 tsp ground cardamom*
- ◆ *2 tsp baking soda*
- ◆ *100 g/4 oz unsalted butter, softened*
- ◆ *225 g/8 oz dark brown sugar*
- ◆ *4 eggs at room temperature, separated*
- ◆ *100 ml/4 fl oz Greek- or Bulgarian-style yoghurt*
- ◆ *100 ml/4 fl oz cottage cheese*
- ◆ *1 tbsp freshly grated orange rind*
- ◆ *275 g/10 oz plain flour*
- ◆ *1/2 tsp salt*
- ◆ *65 g/2 1/2 oz raisins*
- ◆ *175 g/6 oz ready-to-eat dates, stoned and finely chopped*
- ◆ *100 g/4 oz walnuts, finely chopped*

Place 225 ml/8 fl oz honey, the cinnamon, nutmeg and
cardamom in a saucepan and bring to the boil over medium
heat, stirring with a wooden spoon. Stir in the baking soda
and remove from the heat. Cool.

In a large bowl, beat together the butter and brown sugar
until the mixture is fluffy. Beat in the egg yolks, one at a time,
then slowly stir in the cooled honey mixture. In another bowl,
combine the yoghurt, cottage cheese and grated orange rind.

Sift the flour and salt into the honey-egg mixture,
alternating with the yoghurt mixture, stirring after each
addition. Retain 50 g/2 oz of the flour and toss it in a bowl
with the raisins, dates and walnuts. Then stir this dry mixture
into the batter.

Preheat the oven to 150°C/300°F/Gas Mark 2. Beat the
egg whites in a bowl until they hold stiff peaks. Whisk 2 tbsp
egg white into the batter, then gently fold in the remainder.

Pour the batter into a well buttered 25 cm/10 in tube or
kugelhumf tin, lined with buttered greaseproof paper. Bake
the cake for 1 1/2 hours, or until a cocktail stick comes out clean.

Cool the cake in the tin on a rack for 15 minutes, then invert
on to the rack and remove the paper. Brush the cake with
15 ml/1 tbsp honey and allow to cool completely before storing
in an airtight container for at least 2 days before serving.

CRIMEAN ALMOND SQUARES

SEVASTOPOLSKOYE PYECHENYE

◆ ◆ ◆

These biscuit-cakes became popular in Britain following the siege of Sebastopol (1854–55), one of the most bloody episodes of the Crimean War.

MAKES 16 SQUARES

- ◆ *225 g/8 oz plain flour*
- ◆ *75 g/3 oz icing sugar*
- ◆ *salt*
- ◆ *150 g/5 oz unsalted butter*
- ◆ *1 large egg, beaten*

For the topping

- ◆ *6 egg whites*
- ◆ *275 g/10 oz light brown sugar*
- ◆ *¹/₄ tsp ground cinnamon*
- ◆ *¹/₄ tsp finely grated lemon rind*
- ◆ *225 g/8 oz flaked almonds*

Sift the flour into a large bowl and stir in the sugar and a pinch of salt. Cut in the butter and work with your hands until the mixture has the consistency of fine breadcrumbs. Add the egg and stir until the mixture forms into a dough. Roll the dough in a little flour, wrap in cling film and chill for 1 hour.

Roll out the dough into a large square on floured greaseproof paper until it is as thin as possible. Trim the dough on the paper until it measures 30 x 30 cm/12 x 12 in, then fit the paper and rolled dough into a 25 x 25 cm/10 x 10 in baking tin. Push down the dough until you have a small rim (about 1 cm/¹/₂ in). Prick the pastry all over with a fork and chill for 1 hour.

Preheat the oven to 190°C/375°F/Gas Mark 5. Bake the pastry blind for 15 minutes by lining it with greased aluminium foil and weighting it down with baking beans or rice. Remove the baking beans or rice and the foil and bake for a further 5–8 minutes, or until the pastry is light gold. Leave to cool in the tin on a wire rack for 15 minutes, then lift out the pastry, remove from the lining paper and place on a baking tray.

In a saucepan, combine the egg whites, sugar, cinnamon, lemon rind and almonds. Stir gently over high heat, without letting it boil, until the mixture is thickened and starts to become opaque. Pour the mixture into the pastry shell and bake for a further 25 minutes, or until the filling is set and browned. Serve warm or at room temperature, cut into squares.

From Sunny Lands Between the Seas

Georgia, Armenia and Azerbaijan

The three Transcaucasian Republics have some of the most varied scenery and peoples of the old Soviet network. Today, they are also experiencing some of the most violent upheavals, as decades of repression give way to diverging political aspirations and the re-emergence of long-held rivalries between ethnic and religious groups.

The diversity of these regions has deep historical roots, since the lands have been successively fought over by Greeks, Romans, Persians, Byzantines, Arabs, Tartars, Turks and hundreds of smaller tribal groups, in turns rebuffed and assimilated by the native Caucasians (whose descendents are primarily Georgians) and Indo-Europeans (today mainly Armenians). This unsettled background is recognized by the contemporary existence of minority enclaves, the larger masquerading as 'autonomous oblasts' – such as Nagorny-Karabakh in Azerbaijan and South Ossetia on the borders of Georgia – and the smaller enduring less publicized, but often as abrasive, relations with their neighbours.

In the uncertain present this cultural and religious *mélange* has proved a recipe for political and social disaster, but in happier times the fertile landbridge between the Black and Caspian Seas has guaranteed its varied inhabitants an example of the good life much

Armenian brandy is always checked carefully for colour, bouquet and taste.

envied by other Soviet states, who have to pay top prices for Caucasian produce exported to the markets of Moscow, St Petersburg and other urban centres. In the Russian popular view it is an exotic paradise full of sunshine, plenty and the whiff of spice, whose citizens, even under the most oppressive regimes, have always engineered things their own way. Such is their confident spirit in these changing times that while Armenia and Azerbaijan have elected to stay within the new CIS, Georgia has decided to go her own way.

On the face of it, Georgia certainly has the most going for it of the three. It is the least culturally fractured – albeit riven, like the other two, by cataclysmic earthquakes. The rugged beauty of the Georgian countryside is complemented by the bounty of game – mountain goat, deer, boar, partridge, quail and mountain turkey – while the streams meandering through mountain gorges and the limpid lakes shelter trout, carp, barbel and the secretive *kramuli*, found only there. Wild and cultivated fruit grows in profusion; vegetables could be champion entries in any fair in the West, yet lose nothing of their succulence and flavour with their size. The fame of Georgian wine has assured that it is one product associated with the region in the international subconscious.

Georgians tend to be proud, clever and high-spirited; they love feasting and merrymaking but do not suffer fools gladly. Traditional houses are bright in pastel shades; this – together with the frequency of classical columns – gives them a character strangely reminiscent of ancient Cretan reconstructions, except for the wooden galleries running round the upper stories. In summer, there are vine-shaded corners with tables permanently erected for impromptu visits from family and friends – always an occasion for eating and drinking.

Armenia is achingly beautiful too, if perhaps more austerely so; only 1 per cent of its land is lower than 1000 m (3280 ft) above sea level. Disasters, natural and man-made, have stalked its history, so its people have had to be survivors. Their business acumen has stood them in good stead in their diaspora throughout Europe and America – a flight prompted by pogroms in their ancestral homelands, which stretch across the Turkish border, and by closure

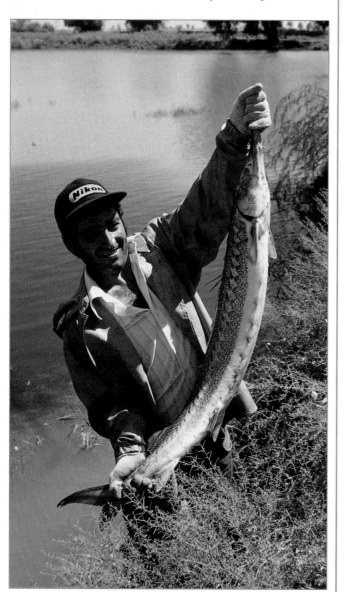

A triumphant Azerbaijani fisherman holds aloft a sturgeon netted in the Caspian Sea.

of their schools, newspapers and churches by the Soviet authorities. Famed as farmers, stonemasons and horsebreeders at home, they have won a reputation as antique dealers, jewellers, haberdashers and restaurateurs abroad.

Both Armenia and Georgia have their own national Orthodox churches with similarly ornate, if distinct, liturgies, though there are also a large number of Armenian Catholics, who follow the Orthodox rite but swear allegiance to the Pope.

There are many overt similarities between the cuisines of Georgia and Armenia, which also echo the cooking styles of Turkey, the Balkans and the Middle East. The delight in the combination of colourful vegetables and peppers, most notably in Armenian *ghivetch*; in vegetables and vine leaves stuffed with combinations of meat and/or rice; in the dominance of lamb – and of grilled meats in general; in the popularity of nuts and dried fruits, and of aubergine 'caviar' and pulses (*lobio/loubia*) stewed in herby tomato sauces; in the use of yoghurt in sweet and savoury dishes. Often made from the fermented milk of the water buffalo, it is known as *matsoni* in Georgia and *matsun* in Armenia.

But there are subtle, and more apparent, differences within these general tastes. While Georgian pilafs are usually made with rice, those of Armenia as often contain cracked wheat (*bulgur*). Both nationalities love walnuts – but for the Georgians they are a passion. Armenians might well replace them in a recipe with pinenuts. The flat cracker bread, known as *lavash* in Armenia, adds an 'i' in Georgia (*lavashi*) as well as yeast to become a puffy bread in the Lebanese and Syrian tradition. The Georgian taste for wild foods is satisfied by nettles and sarsaparilla in soups and wild purslane (*donduri*) in salads; the sour-sweet tang of tarragon can often be detected in their favourite dishes. Armenians look to pumpkin, pomegranate and sesame seeds to provide a special fillip to food, while the slightly acrid bite of coriander supplants that of tarragon. And while the Georgians toast their happiness in wine and champagne, the Armenians raise their brandy glasses.

The republic of Azerbaijan is an impressionistic mixture of traditions, and one that has seen little of non-Russian tourism. Though ethnically and linguistically Turkish, its style of life is a reflection of that in Central Asia on the other side of the Caspian Sea. Its food, on the other hand, borrows liberally from both the Georgian and Central Asian traditions. *Pilaf* and lamb kebab (*shashlyk*) recall the former, while yoghurt soups and dumplings have an Uzbek flavour. And, as in Uzbekistan, social life in Muslim Azerbaijan revolves largely around the teahouse or *chaikhana*.

General view of the 16th to 18th century temples and fortress at Annanuri in rural Georgia.

ONION, LENTIL AND LEMON SOUP

SUP IZ LUKA, GOROKHA I LIMONA

◆ ◆ ◆

Barley and lentils are two Armenian favourites paired in this earthy soup. Served with warm cornbread it would make a filling supper or lunch.

SERVES 6

◆ *225 ml/8 fl oz water*
◆ *75 g/3 oz pearl barley*
◆ *15 ml/1 tbsp tomato purée*
◆ *1.5 litres/2$\frac{1}{2}$ pt beef stock*
◆ *175 g/6 oz brown lentils, rinsed and picked over*
◆ *5 onions, sliced very thinly*
◆ *1 tsp dried anise seeds*

◆ *juice of 1 large lemon*
◆ *large pinch of sweet paprika*
◆ *pinch of cayenne pepper*
◆ *salt and freshly ground black pepper*
◆ *12 paper-thin lemon slices*

Bring the water to the boil in a large enamelled or stainless steel saucepan. Stir in the barley, cover, and simmer over low heat for about 20–25 minutes, until the barley is just tender and the water has been absorbed. Stir in the tomato purée, beef stock, lentils, onions and anise. Bring to the boil, cover, and simmer over low heat for 1 hour, or until the lentils are soft.

Stir in the lemon juice, paprika, cayenne pepper and salt and pepper to taste and simmer uncovered for a further 20 minutes. Pour the soup into heated bowls and garnish each with two very thin slices of lemon.

SPICED PUMPKIN SOUP

TYKVENNY SUP Z PRYANOSTYAMI

◆ ◆ ◆

Pumpkins grow in profusion throughout the southern states of the former Soviet Union. They are a cheap source of vitamins, and are served baked, stewed, stuffed, in pastries and in soups like this Armenian speciality. Nothing is wasted – even the seeds are roasted and treated as snack food or a condiment to sprinkle over dishes. The yoghurt in this soup would be *matsun*, made from water-buffalo milk.

SERVES 8

- ◆ *3 tbsp pumpkin seeds*
- ◆ *45 ml/3 tbsp vegetable oil*
- ◆ *50 g/2 oz currants*
- ◆ *675 g/1½ lb leeks, trimmed, halved and thinly sliced*
- ◆ *2 medium carrots, peeled and finely chopped*
- ◆ *675 g/1½ lb fresh pumpkin, peeled, seeded, fibre removed and cubed*
- ◆ *1 litre/1¾ pt chicken stock*
- ◆ *425 ml/¾ pt milk*
- ◆ *¼ tsp allspice*
- ◆ *150 ml/5 fl oz yoghurt*

Preheat the oven to 200°C/400°F/Gas Mark 6. Place the pumpkin seeds on a baking tray and toast in the oven for 5–6 minutes, or until they are golden. Set aside.

Heat the oil in a saucepan and stir the currants over medium heat until they are puffed and glossy. Transfer with a slotted spoon to a plate and set aside. Stir the leeks and carrots into the pan and cook over low heat for 10 minutes, then add the pumpkin cubes and stir-fry for another 10 minutes until the leeks are lightly coloured. Add 425 ml/¾ pt chicken stock. Cover and cook the vegetables for 20 minutes, or until the pumpkin is softened.

In a blender or food processor, purée the vegetable mixture in batches until smooth. Return the purée to the saucepan and stir in the remaining stock, the milk and the allspice. Cook over medium heat, covered, for 15 minutes, stirring occasionally. Stir in the currants just before serving.

Serve the soup in individual bowls. Top each serving with a swirl of yoghurt and sprinkle over some toasted pumpkin seeds.

SOUR CHICKEN SOUP

CHIKHIRTMA

◆ ◆ ◆

A traditional Georgian soup, this has echoes of Syria, Israel and the Indian subcontinent in it. If a thicker, more stew-like result is wanted, the chicken can be shredded into the broth, but this version is more like that commonly encountered in Tbilisi *kafes* and *restorans*.

SERVES 8

- ◆ *1.75 kg/4 lb chicken, gutted and cleaned*
- ◆ *1 whole onion, unpeeled*
- ◆ *1 celery stick*
- ◆ *3–4 saffron threads*
- ◆ *5 black peppercorns, crushed*
- ◆ *pinch of cayenne pepper*
- ◆ *3 eggs*
- ◆ *2 egg yolks*
- ◆ *25 g/1 oz unsalted butter*
- ◆ *2 onions, finely chopped*
- ◆ *1 tbsp flour*
- ◆ *100 ml/4 fl oz fresh lemon juice*
- ◆ *2 tbsp finely chopped fresh coriander*
- ◆ *2 tbsp finely chopped fresh parsley*
- ◆ *1 tbsp finely chopped fresh mint*
- ◆ *salt and freshly ground black pepper*

Place the chicken, whole onion and celery stick in a heavy saucepan. Add cold water to cover well and bring to the boil over high heat. Add the saffron, peppercorns and cayenne pepper to taste, then cover and lower the heat to minimum. Simmer gently for 1½ hours, or until the bird is tender but not falling to pieces. During cooking, skim the scum from the top of the stock occasionally.

Transfer the chicken to a dish to drain. Add the juices to the stock. Reserve the bird for another use, serving it with Spiced Walnut Sauce or using it in Russian Chicken and Potato Salad.

Remove the peppercorns and any bits from the stock with a small sieve, but keep it simmering. In a large bowl, lightly beat together the eggs and egg yolks. Melt the butter in a frying pan over medium heat. Sauté the onions until they are softened and just coloured, about 6–8 minutes. Add the flour and stir for 3 minutes. Add 275 ml/10 fl oz stock to the frying pan and stir until it begins to thicken. Take off the heat and allow to rest for 2 minutes, then pour the thickened mixture slowly into the eggs, beating all the time. In turn, pour the egg and stock mixture and the lemon juice into the rest of the stock, beating gently over low heat so that it does not curdle. Stir in the chopped herbs, season the soup to taste and serve immediately.

GROUND SPICED WALNUT SAUCE

SATSIVI

◆ ◆ ◆

This is the best-known classic sauce of the Georgian repertoire, although it is probably more familiar in its Turkish incarnation, Circassian Sauce. As in Turkey, it is usually paired with poached chicken, but the addition of breadcrumbs and higher spicing in the Turkish version results in a less vibrant sauce than the recipe below.

MAKES ABOUT 600 ML/1 PT

- ◆ *175 g/6 oz shelled walnuts*
- ◆ *4 cloves garlic, crushed and chopped*
- ◆ *350 ml/12 fl oz chicken stock*
- ◆ *25 g/1 oz chicken fat or clarified butter*
- ◆ *2 medium onions, finely chopped*
- ◆ *1 bay leaf*
- ◆ *½ tsp coriander seeds*
- ◆ *¼ tsp cinnamon*
- ◆ *¼ tsp turmeric*
- ◆ *large pinch of ground cloves*
- ◆ *large pinch of cayenne pepper*
- ◆ *30 ml/2 tbsp red wine vinegar*
- ◆ *salt and freshly ground black pepper*
- ◆ *2 tsp finely chopped tarragon*
- ◆ *2 tsp finely chopped flat-leaved parsley*

In a food processor fitted with the metal blade, process the nuts and garlic until they are as smooth as possible (or grind by hand using a mortar and pestle). Add 5 ml/1 tsp chicken stock, if needed.

In a heavy enamelled or stainless steel saucepan, melt the chicken fat or clarified butter. Cook the onions over low heat until softened but not coloured, about 5 minutes. Stir in the walnut-garlic mixture, the bay leaf and the chicken stock. Bring to the boil, then lower the heat and simmer for 15 minutes, until reduced and thickened. Stir in the spices, vinegar, seasoning to taste and 1 tsp each of the herbs, reserving the rest. Transfer to a bowl to cool, then chill for 2 hours. Serve with the remaining herbs scattered over.

SAUCES

BAKU TOMATO PRESERVE

KONSERVIROVANNYE TOMATY PO-BAKINSKY

◆ ◆ ◆

This highly-flavoured chutney is a good accompaniment to the fish and lamb dishes common to the Azerbaijani and Georgian regions.

MAKES ABOUT 600 ML/1 PT

- ◆ *1 red sweet pepper, cored, seeded and finely chopped*
- ◆ *1 yellow sweet pepper, cored, seeded and finely chopped*
- ◆ *2 thin green hot chillies, seeded, trimmed and finely chopped*
- ◆ *2 beefsteak tomatoes,*
- *skinned, cored, seeded and chopped*
- ◆ *1 onion, chopped*
- ◆ *1 tsp sugar*
- ◆ *salt*
- ◆ *15 ml/1 tbsp red wine vinegar*

Combine all the ingredients in a glass or pottery bowl and mix well. Cover with cling film and leave to marinate for 3–24 hours.

GEORGIAN POMEGRANATE CHUTNEY

GRUZINSKAYA GRANATOVAYA PODLIVKA

◆ ◆ ◆

This pomegranate chutney is delicious with fish and with grilled lamb.

MAKES ABOUT 225 ML/8 FL OZ

- ◆ *Seeds from 2 medium pomegranates*
- ◆ *1 orange, peeled, pith removed and cut into pieces*
- ◆ *10 ml/2 tsp fresh lime or lemon juice*
- ◆ *2 spring onions, trimmed and finely chopped*
- ◆ *¹/₄ tsp mixed cayenne pepper and sweet paprika*
- ◆ *2 tsp finely chopped fresh hot chilli*
- ◆ *1 tbsp finely chopped fresh coriander*

Combine all the ingredients in a glass or pottery bowl and stir to mix thoroughly. Cover and chill for 3–12 hours.

GEORGIAN CHEESE-FILLED BREADS

KHACHAPURI

◆ ◆ ◆

This delicious bread is made in a variety of ways in its home territory. Round, filled loaves are probably the most common presentation, while some other versions have layered pastry. These open-faced 'buns' are easily frozen if they are not all needed at once. In Georgia the cheese used would be *suluguni*, a cheese rather like Turkish *halloumi*.

MAKES ABOUT 16–18

- ◆ 65 g/2¹/₂ oz unsalted butter, softened
- ◆ 100 ml/4 fl oz lukewarm water
- ◆ 2¹/₂ tsp (1 x 8 g/¹/₄ oz packet) active dry yeast
- ◆ 2 tsp sugar
- ◆ 275 g/10 oz plain flour

- ◆ 1 tsp salt
- ◆ 450 g/1 lb halloumi cheese, grated
- ◆ 2 eggs
- ◆ 2 tbsp finely chopped oregano, marjoram or tarragon

In a small saucepan, heat 45 g/1¹/₂ oz butter over a low heat until only just melted. Allow to cool.

Place the water in a small bowl and sprinkle the yeast and sugar into it. Leave for 15 minutes in a warm place, or until foamy. In a large bowl, mix together 225 g/8 oz flour and the salt. Make a well in the centre and pour in the yeast and the melted butter; stir with a fork until you have a pliable dough.

Transfer the dough to a floured surface and knead with your hands for 5 minutes, adding the remaining flour as you work the dough. When the dough is no longer sticky but smooth and still soft, transfer it to a well-buttered bowl and turn it to coat with the butter. Leave it to rise in a warm place, covered with cling film, for about 1 hour, or until doubled in size.

In another bowl, stir together the grated cheese, 1 egg and the remaining softened butter. Work the mixture well with your hands and set aside.

Knock back the dough, halve it and roll one half into a 40 x 20 cm/16 x 8 in rectangle. Divide the rectangle into squares. Use half the cheese mixture to make mounds in the centre of the squares and fold the sides up around and slightly over the mixture, pulling out the corners slightly. Repeat with remaining dough and cheese mixture.

Preheat the oven to 190°C/375°F/Gas Mark 5. Make an egg wash by mixing the remaining egg with a little water in a small bowl. Arrange the filled bread cases on two baking trays and brush with the egg wash. Allow them to rest for 15 minutes in a warm place, then bake in the oven for 20–25 minutes, or until they are golden and the cheese is toasted. Transfer to a rack, sprinkle with the fresh herbs and leave to cool for 15 minutes before serving warm. (The *khachapuri* may be frozen and reheated at the same temperature for 25 minutes from frozen.)

KARABAKH SALAD

SALAT PO-KARABAKHSKY

◆ ◆ ◆

This light mixed salad is characteristic of the eastern reaches of the Caucasian Republic which borders on the Caspian Sea. The Armenian version is almost the same, but substitutes 2 tomatoes for the radishes.

SERVES 4

◆ 1 bunch of radishes, trimmed and thinly sliced
◆ 1 small cucumber, peeled, seeded and thinly sliced
◆ 3 spring onions, trimmed and chopped
◆ 2 tsp finely chopped fresh mint
◆ 45 ml/3 tbsp fresh lemon juice
◆ 45 ml/3 tbsp olive oil
◆ salt and freshly ground black pepper
◆ 100 g/4 oz fresh ewe's or feta cheese, cubed

Combine the radishes, cucumber, spring onions and fresh mint in an attractive bowl. Whisk the lemon juice and oil together and season to taste. Pour over the salad and toss gently. Scatter the cubes of cheese around the edges of the bowl and serve immediately.

Stuffed Vine Leaves

STUFFED VINE LEAVES

YARPAKH DOLMASY

◆ ◆ ◆

**Both Armenians and Georgians love stuffed vine leaves –
with or without meat. The Armenians are more likely
to use *bulgur* rather than rice.**

MAKES ABOUT 30

- ◆ 100 g/4 oz coarse bulgur (cracked wheat)
- ◆ 425 ml/³/₄ pt hot water
- ◆ 2 packets vine leaves in brine (about 30 leaves)
- ◆ 50 ml/2 fl oz olive oil
- ◆ 50 g/2 oz pine nuts
- ◆ 2 small onions, finely chopped
- ◆ 225 g/8 oz lean minced lamb
- ◆ 50 g/2 oz currants
- ◆ 50 g/2 oz ready-to-eat dried apricots, finely chopped
- ◆ 2 tbsp chopped fresh dill
- ◆ 2 tbsp chopped fresh mint
- ◆ salt and freshly ground black pepper
- ◆ 65 ml/2¹/₂ fl oz lemon juice
- ◆ 225 ml/8 fl oz chicken stock
- ◆ 2–3 lemons, quartered
- ◆ 600 ml/1 pt Greek- or Bulgarian-style yoghurt
- ◆ ground cinnamon

Place the bulgur in a large bowl and add the hot water. Leave to soak for 30 minutes.

Meanwhile place the vine leaves in another large bowl, cover them with cold water and leave them to soak for 20 minutes, or until they will pull apart easily. Drain, pour fresh water into the bowl, and drain again thoroughly. Spread the vine leaves out and pat them dry with absorbent kitchen paper. Drain the bulgur in a fine sieve or through muslin.

Heat the oil in a heavy frying pan over moderate heat. Add the pine nuts and toast, stirring, until golden. Transfer with a slotted spoon to a plate and set aside. Add the onions to the oil and sauté gently until they are soft and just colouring, about 8 minutes. Add the lamb and sauté, until browned. Add the currants, apricots, herbs, seasoning to taste, pine nuts, bulgar and lemon juice; heat until warmed through.

Take a vine leaf and place it stem-side facing you on a flat surface. Spoon a scant tbsp of stuffing in the centre of the leaf. Trim off the stem, tuck the sides over the filling and roll away from you to form a tight, neat roll. Repeat with the remaining stuffing and leaves. Arrange the stuffed rolls, seam-side down, in a flameproof casserole large enough to take them in one tight layer. Add the stock and enough hot water to come halfway up the sides of the rolls. Place the casserole over high heat and bring to the boil. Cover, and simmer over minimum heat for about 40 minutes.

Remove from the heat, uncover, and let the rolls cool to room temperature, then chill if desired. (The rolls will keep in the refrigerator, well-covered with cling film, for 3 days).

Serve the rolls garnished with lemon quarters and with a bowl of thick yoghurt sprinkled with cinnamon.

SPINACH AND WALNUT PURÉE

PKHALA

◆ ◆ ◆

**This spiced spinach dish is a common offering at
Georgian *zakuska* tables. Armenians substitute lemon juice
and toasted pine nuts for the vinegar and walnuts. It is
scooped up in flat, flaky *lavashi* (or Armenian *lavash*) bread,
with yoghurt accompanying it if desired.**

SERVES 4–6

- ◆ 1.5 kg/3 lb spinach leaves, washed and coarse stems removed
- ◆ 1 small onion, chopped
- ◆ 15 ml/1 tbsp olive oil
- ◆ 3 cloves garlic, crushed
- ◆ 5 threads saffron
- ◆ 15 ml/1 tbsp hot water
- ◆ 50 g/2 oz fresh coriander, coarse stems removed
- ◆ 50 g/2 oz fresh flat-leaved parsley, coarse stems removed
- ◆ 30 ml/2 tbsp red wine vinegar or lemon juice
- ◆ 75 g/3 oz shelled walnuts or toasted pine nuts
- ◆ salt and freshly ground black pepper
- ◆ 150 ml/¹/₄ pt chicken stock
- ◆ extra chopped walnuts or toasted whole pine nuts

Place the spinach in a large saucepan and cook in the moisture clinging to its leaves, stirring occasionally, until it is wilted – about 8 minutes. Squeeze the spinach to remove as much water as possible and allow to drain further.

In a frying pan, sauté the onion in the olive oil until it is soft. Stir in the garlic and cook over medium heat for 2–3 more minutes, but do not let the garlic brown. Meanwhile, soak the saffron threads in the hot water.

Squeeze the spinach again to remove excess water and chop it coarsely. In a blender or processor, combine the spinach, the contents of the frying pan and the fresh coriander and parsley. Process until smooth. Transfer to a bowl, together with the saffron and its liquid, and the vinegar or lemon juice.

Using the grinder attachment of the blender or the cleaned bowl of the food processor, process the walnuts or pine nuts until finely chopped but not mashed. Stir into the spinach mixture with seasoning and as much of the chicken stock as is needed to make a stiffish purée. Spoon the purée into a serving dish, smooth the top with the prongs of a fork, and leave to stand, covered with cling film, for at least 3 hours for the flavours to combine. Scatter over a handful of chopped walnuts or toasted pine nuts just before serving.

POOR MAN'S CAVIAR

BAKLAZHANNYA IKRA

◆ ◆ ◆

The smoky flavour of this Georgian 'caviar' has become familiar to Westerners through Lebanese and Turkish restaurants which also serve versions of this classic dip. An Armenian version, known as *babaghanouj*, adds green pepper and pomegranate seeds, shown as options below.

SERVES 6

- ◆ 1 kg/2 lb aubergines, trimmed and halved lengthways
- ◆ salt and freshly ground black pepper
- ◆ 50 ml/4 tbsp olive oil
- ◆ 5 spring onions, trimmed and finely chopped
- ◆ 1 green sweet pepper, cored, seeded and chopped (optional)
- ◆ 2 cloves garlic, crushed and finely chopped
- ◆ 2 ripe tomatoes, skinned, seeded and chopped
- ◆ pinch of cayenne pepper
- ◆ 15 ml/1 tbsp fresh lemon juice
- ◆ 3 tbsp finely chopped fresh coriander or parsley
- ◆ seeds from 1 pomegranate (optional)

Slash the aubergines on the sides and sprinkle with salt all over. Place in a colander and let them drain for 30 minutes. Rinse the aubergines and pat them dry with absorbent kitchen paper.

Preheat the oven to 190°C/375°F/Gas mark 5. Place the aubergines on a baking tray, cut side down, and brush all over with oil. Bake in the oven for 40 minutes, until very tender. Remove from the oven to cool.

Meanwhile, place 30 ml/2 tbsp olive oil in a frying pan. Add the spring onions and the green pepper if used and stir for 5 minutes until soft. Add the garlic and cook for another minute.

When the aubergine is cool, scrape out the flesh and chop it finely. Add the rest of the oil to the pan and stir in the chopped aubergine, together with the tomatoes, cayenne pepper and seasoning to taste. Turn the heat to high and bring the mixture to boiling point, mashing and stirring it at the same time. Cover, lower the heat and simmer, stirring occasionally, for about 30 minutes, or until the mixture has thickened and most of the moisture has evaporated. Stir in the lemon juice and coriander (substitute parsley and add the pomegranate seeds if making *babaghanouj*), adjust the seasoning and transfer the mixture to a bowl to cool. Leave to stand for at least 3 hours; serve at room temperature. (The caviar may be kept, chilled, for up to 3 days.)

TRANSCAUCASIAN CABBAGE AND MINT SALAD

TRANSCARKAZSKY SALAT IZ KAPUSTY Z MYATOY

◆ ◆ ◆

Cabbage is a staple of the former Soviet Union, but in the south the spicing is notably different, and sour cream gives way to yoghurt, when used. This is a cool, refreshing 'coleslaw' served as a *zakuska* or to accompany a picnic or outdoor meal.

SERVES 6-8

- ◆ 23 ml/1¹/₂ tbsp lemon juice
- ◆ 30 ml/2 tbsp white wine vinegar
- ◆ 23 ml/1¹/₂ tbsp sunflower or olive oil
- ◆ ¹/₂ tsp sugar
- ◆ freshly ground black pepper
- ◆ 1 large red onion
- ◆ 1.25 kg/2¹/₂ lb white Dutch cabbage, outer leaves removed, cored, quartered and finely shredded
- ◆ 6 tbsp finely shredded fresh mint leaves

Beat together the lemon juice and vinegar in a large bowl. Whisk in the oil, sugar and a generous dash of pepper. Halve and finely slice all but one-quarter of the red onion. Stir the onion slices into the dressing and wrap the remaining section in aluminium foil. Then gently toss the shredded cabbage and mint leaves in the dressing. Combine thoroughly and chill for at least 3 hours.

Just before serving, slice the reserved onion and sprinkle over the salad.

ARMENIAN VEGETABLE STEW

GHIVETCH

◆ ◆ ◆

**There are no hard and fast rules to making this very
Armenian speciality. It can contain meat to make it more
substantial – tender pieces of lamb sautéed before adding the
vegetables – while the latter are an amalgam of whatever is in
the garden, for example, substitute turnip for carrots,
cabbage for celery.**

SERVES 4–6

- ◆ 75 ml/3 fl oz olive oil
- ◆ 4 cloves garlic, crushed
- ◆ 225 ml/8 fl oz beef stock
  or consommé
- ◆ 1 bay leaf
- ◆ $^1/_2$ tsp dried tarragon
- ◆ $^1/_2$ tsp dried oregano
- ◆ salt and freshly ground
  black pepper

- ◆ 2 medium carrots, halved
  and thinly sliced
- ◆ 100 g/4 oz fresh stringless
  green beans, cut into
  1 cm/$^1/_2$ in lengths
- ◆ 2 small potatoes, peeled
  and diced
- ◆ 2 celery sticks, halved
  lengthways and thinly
  sliced

- ◆ 1 courgette, thinly sliced
  into rounds
- ◆ 1 small aubergine, halved
  and thinly sliced
- ◆ 1 small red onion, thinly
  sliced
- ◆ 1 small cauliflower,
  broken into florets

- ◆ $^1/_2$ red sweet pepper, cored,
  seeded and cut into strips
- ◆ $^1/_2$ green sweet pepper,
  cored, seeded and cut
  into strips
- ◆ 75 g/3 oz shelled fresh peas

Preheat the oven to 180°C/350°F/Gas Mark 4. Place the oil in a
large enamelled or stainless steel casserole and warm it over
medium heat. Add the garlic and stir to flavour the oil, about
2 minutes. Pour in the beef stock or consommé and add the
bay leaf, herbs and seasoning to taste. Bring to the boil.

Add the vegetables, little by little, stirring to combine as you
add them. Cover the casserole with a lid or foil and transfer to
the oven. Bake for about 1 hour or until the vegetables are all
tender, stirring occasionally. Serve as a vegetarian main
course or as a side dish.

FISH

SEVAN LAKE TROUT YEREVAN-STYLE
SEVANSKAYA FOREL PO-YEREVANSKY
◆ ◆ ◆

**Said to be the most delicious in Armenia, Sevan Lake
trout can sometimes be found in the market at Yerevan,
70 km/46 miles to the southwest of the lake. The capital's
market is richer in vegetables and herbs than is the norm.
This recipe combines the flavours of that region, though
we cannot duplicate the unique lake fish.**

SERVES 4

- *4 375 g/12 oz brown or rainbow trout, cleaned and gutted*
- *salt and freshly ground black pepper*
- *50 g/2 oz unsalted butter*
- *225 g/8 oz bottled artichoke hearts in oil*
- *50 g/2 oz plain flour*
- *150 ml/¹/₄ pt fresh lemon juice*
- *225 ml/8 fl oz water*
- *75 ml 3 fl oz vegetable oil*
- *23 ml/1¹/₂ tbsp dry white wine*
- *3 tbsp drained capers*
- *3 tbsp finely chopped fresh flat-leaved parsley*
- *pinch of sweet paprika*
- *small pinch of cayenne pepper*

Rinse the trout and pat it dry with absorbent kitchen paper.
Season to taste and set aside.

In a heavy saucepan over low heat, gently melt the butter until the solids have sunk to the bottom of the pan. Slowly pour off the clarified butter on the top and set aside. Discard the white residue and wash the pan.

Pour the oil from the bottled artichokes into the saucepan. Add 1 tsp flour and heat over a medium flame, stirring. Slowly add half the lemon juice and the water and bring the liquid to the boil, whisking. Lower the heat to simmer, stir in the artichoke hearts and cook, uncovered, for about 10 minutes, or until the sauce is reduced and thickened. Set aside.

Preheat the oven to 190°C/375°F/Gas Mark 5. Dredge the trout in flour and shake off the excess. Heat half the oil in a frying pan, and brown two of the trout on one side only. Remove to a roasting tin lined with oiled foil, add the rest of the oil to the frying pan and brown the two remaining trout on one side. Transfer to the roasting tin. Bake the trout for 10 minutes, or until the flesh is opaque and just beginning to flake. Carefully fillet the trout, arrange on four warmed serving plates, and sprinkle the fillets with the wine.

Stir the remaining lemon juice, the clarified butter and the capers into the sauce and heat through. Spoon the mixture over the fillets and sprinkle with the chopped parsley and the spices. Serve immediately.

ARMENIAN CHICKEN AND CHICKPEA STEW

TYSHYONY TSYPLYONOK Z GRUSHAMI PO-ARMYANSKY

◆ ◆ ◆

The Armenians have a spicy condiment sold as Aintab Red Pepper here in the West. Since it is difficult to find, two thin medium-hot red peppers have been substituted here.

SERVES 6

- 4 threads saffron
- 90 ml/3$^{1}/_{2}$ fl oz hot water
- 10 cloves garlic, crushed
- 2 fresh thin medium-hot red peppers, seeded and chopped
- 60 ml/4 tbsp vegetable or sunflower oil
- 1.5 kg/3 lb chicken breasts and thighs, washed and dried
- salt and freshly ground black pepper
- 2 tbsp ground coriander
- 1 tsp dried oregano
- 2 x 400 g/14 oz cans plum tomatoes, drained
- 425 ml/3$/_{4}$ pt water
- 575 g/1$^{1}/_{4}$ lb can chickpeas, drained
- 30 ml/2 tbsp lemon juice

Soak the saffron in hot water for 10 minutes. Place the saffron and liquid, garlic and peppers in a blender or food processor. Process until finely chopped and set aside.

Heat the oil in a casserole over medium-hot heat. Season the chicken to taste and sauté in batches until lightly browned. Remove to a plate and keep warm.

Reduce the heat and add the garlic purée. Stir with a wooden spoon for 2 minutes, then add the ground coriander and oregano. Stir for a further 2 minutes, then add the tomatoes. Break them up with the spoon while cooking for 3 minutes, then add the water. Add the chicken pieces and spoon the sauce over them. Bring to the boil, cover, and simmer over low heat for 20 minutes.

Add the chickpeas and continue to cook, covered, for a further 15 minutes. Remove the lid, stir in the lemon juice and increase the heat. Boil for 5 minutes to reduce the sauce. Serve immediately.

GEORGIAN LAMB CUBES ON SKEWERS

SHASHLYK

◆ ◆ ◆

Shashlyk is the Georgian name for what is more commonly known here by its Turkish title, *shish kebab*. Unlike the Muslims, however, the Orthodox Georgians marinate their lamb in their dry Telliani wine.

SERVES 6

- ◆ *1 onion, chopped*
- ◆ *50 ml/2 fl oz mixed olive oil and vegetable oil*
- ◆ *1 bay leaf*
- ◆ *1 clove garlic, crushed*
- ◆ *2 tbsp finely chopped flat-leaved parsley*
- ◆ *1 tsp dried oregano*
- ◆ *¼ tsp freshly ground black pepper*
- ◆ *large pinch cayenne pepper*
- ◆ *225 ml/8 fl oz dry red wine*
- ◆ *1 kg/2 lb lean boneless leg of lamb steak, cubed*
- ◆ *30 small white onions, peeled*
- ◆ *2 small red sweet peppers, cored, seeded and cut into square pieces*

Place the onion, oils, bay leaf, garlic, parsley, oregano, pepper and cayenne pepper in a thick plastic bag. Pour in the wine.

Pheasant Georgian-style

Phazan po-Gruzinsky

◆ ◆ ◆

This dish is a relative of Walnut Chicken but has its own special accents. Made in its home region it would use sweet golden Gurdzhanni wine, but Madeira or *oloroso* sherry are acceptable substitutes.

SERVES 4

- *175 ml/6 fl oz boiling water*
- *1 heaped tsp Turkish or other green tea leaves*
- *675 g/1¹/₂ lb green grapes, stems removed*
- *1.25–1.5 kg/2¹/₂–3 lb pheasant, cleaned and trussed*
- *juice of 3 oranges*
- *1 tsp grated orange rind*
- *50 g/2 oz walnuts, chopped*
- *225 ml/8 fl oz Madeira*
- *salt and freshly ground black pepper*
- *45 g/1¹/₂ oz butter*
- *100 ml/4 fl oz game consommé*
- *quince jelly (optional)*

Pour the boiling water over the tea and allow it to steep for 10 minutes, then strain. Set aside the liquid tea and discard the leaves.

In a large bowl, mash the grapes with a potato masher or pestle. Continue until they are a pulpy mass and there is plenty of juice. Strain the mixture, discard the pulp and set aside the juice.

Place the pheasant in a Dutch oven or roasting tin with the orange rind and walnuts. Mix together the tea, grape juice, orange juice and Madeira and pour over the pheasant. Season to taste and dot the bird with butter. Cover with a lid or foil and bring the braising liquid to the boil on top of the stove. Reduce the heat and simmer for 45–50 minutes.

Preheat the oven to 220°C/425°F/Gas Mark 7. Lift out the pheasant and place it on a dish to drain. Strain the cooking liquid into a saucepan and discard the solids. Place the saucepan over medium-high heat and reduce until it is thick and syrupy, about 8 minutes. Carve the bird into serving pieces and return to the roasting tin. Cook uncovered for 20 minutes, or until it has browned lightly.

Transfer the pheasant to a serving dish. Pour the reduced stock over the pieces and serve immediately. Serve accompanied by a bowl of quince jelly, if available.

Hold tightly shut and shake vigorously to combine. Add the cubed lamb, tie the bag closed and place it in a bowl large enough to contain it comfortably. Leave for 24–36 hours in the refrigerator to mature.

Drain the lamb well but reserve the marinade. Thread the pieces on to 6 long skewers, alternating with the onions and red pepper.

Prepare the coals of a barbecue or preheat a grill. When ready, lay the skewers about 13 cm/5 in from the heat. Cook, turning once or twice and basting frequently, for about 10 minutes, or until the lamb is still pink inside but well browned. Serve with rice and Baku Tomato Preserve .

GEORGIAN MEAT AND TOMATO STEW
CHAKHOBILI

◆ ◆ ◆

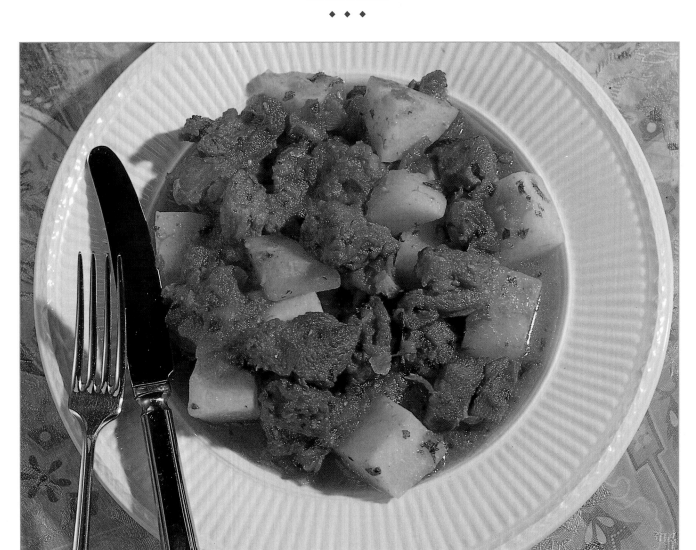

This traditional dish is made as frequently with chicken as it is with lamb. In the old manner, it is cooked in a large iron pot over hot coals, but this version has been adapted to suit the modern hob.

SERVES 6

- ◆ *15 ml/1 tbsp vegetable or olive oil*
- ◆ *1 kg/2 lb lamb steaks, trimmed of fat and cubed*
- ◆ *2 onions, chopped*
- ◆ *675 g/1$\frac{1}{2}$ lb whole Roma or plum tomatoes, skinned, seeded and roughly chopped*
- ◆ *3 large potatoes, peeled and roughly cubed*

- ◆ *salt and freshly ground black pepper*
- ◆ *50 g/2 oz fresh coriander, chopped*
- ◆ *50 g/2 oz fresh flat-leaved parsley, chopped*
- ◆ *5 fresh basil leaves, chopped*
- ◆ *8 cloves garlic, crushed*

Heat the oil in a large enamelled or stainless steel casserole until very hot but not smoking. Tilt to cover the bottom with the oil. Add the lamb pieces and brown, stirring with a wooden spoon, for 10 minutes. When the meat is coloured, add the onions and continue to stir until they are soft. Add the tomatoes and use the spoon to crush them. Stir in the potatoes and seasoning to taste. Cover and simmer over low heat for about 45 minutes or until the meat and potatoes are tender and the tomatoes have become a mushy sauce. Uncover and turn up the heat., Stir in the herbs and garlic and continue to stir as the sauce bubbles for 10 minutes. Take off the heat, cover, and leave to stand for 5–8 minutes before serving.

LOSH KIBBEH KEBABS

LOSH KIBBEHSKIYE KEBABY

◆ ◆ ◆

The Azerbaijani version of this dish dispenses with the *bulgur* and increases the minced meat, but the spices and herbs are much the same. The Armenian version is given here as the *bulgur* gives the dish a more interesting texture.

SERVES 4

- 100 g/4 oz fine bulgur
- 30 ml/2 tbsp tomato purée
- 450 g/1 lb lean minced lamb
- 3 tbsp chopped onion
- 3 tbsp chopped fresh flat-leaved parsley
- $^1/_2$ tsp allspice
- $^1/_4$ tsp cayenne pepper
- salt and freshly ground black pepper
- $^1/_2$ tsp grated lemon rind
- vegetable oil
- 1 small red sweet pepper, cored, seeded and sliced into rounds

Place the *bulgur* in a bowl, add generous water to cover and leave to soak for 10–15 minutes, or until the bulgur is softened but still springy. Drain and dry with absorbent kitchen paper.

Place the *bulgur*, half the tomato purée and half the minced lamb in the bowl of a food processor and process until almost smooth. Transfer to a bowl. Process the remaining lamb and tomato purée with the onion and $^1/_2$ tbsp parsley until that too is as smooth as possible. Transfer to the bowl. Sprinkle with the spices, salt and pepper to taste, and lemon rind. Work the mixture with your hands until everything is well combined.

Dip your hands in cold water and use to form the mixture into long thin sausage shapes. Spear each 'sausage' with a skewer and press the meat around it.

Brush the kebabs with oil and cook about 8 cm/4 in from the coals or grill. Turn the skewers occasionally and cook for about 10–12 minutes. Arrange the kebabs on a serving dish, top with the pepper and scatter with the reserved parsley leaves.

ARMENIAN SEMOLINA PUDDING

ARMYANSKY MANNY PUDDING

◆ ◆ ◆

This semolina pudding displays the extravagant Caucasian sweet tooth which is shared with the Turkish and Levantine cultures.

SERVES 4

- 350 ml/12 fl oz medium white wine
- 500 ml/18 fl oz water
- grated rind of $^1/_2$ lemon
- 550 g/1$^1/_4$ lb sugar
- juice and grated rind of 1 orange
- salt
- 100 g/ 4 oz semolina
- 2 egg yolks
- 3 egg whites
- 5 ml/1 tsp lemon juice
- 25 g/1 oz shelled pistachio nuts

Place the wine, 300 ml/$^1/_2$ pt water and the lemon and orange rind in an enamelled or stainless steel saucepan. Add a pinch of salt and stir over high heat. Bring to the boil and add the semolina to the pan, stirring. Reduce the heat and simmer for about 6 minutes until the mixture is thick and smooth.

Stir 100 g/4 oz sugar and the orange juice into the mixture, and continue stirring until it boils again. Take off the heat and whisk in the egg yolks.

Whisk the egg whites in a bowl until stiff but not dry. Carefully fold into the semolina, little by little, until all the whites are incorporated.

Preheat the oven to 170°C/325°F/Gas Mark 3. Pour the pudding into a fluted mould and place the mould in a tin. Add enough water to come halfway up the sides of the mould. Bake the pudding for 55 minutes, or until set. Remove from the oven and allow to cool slightly.

Meanwhile, make the syrup. Combine 5 ml/1 tsp lemon juice with the remaining water and sugar. Bring to the boil, stirring, until the sugar is dissolved. Continue to cook over lower heat until the liquid has become syrupy. Mix in the pistachio nuts.

Turn the pudding over and carefully unmould on to a serving plate. Spoon a pool of syrup and nuts around the foot of the pudding and over the top. Serve the remainder separately in a sauceboat.

ARMENIAN TOASTED BREAD PUDDING WITH CONDENSED CREAM

EKMEK KAIMAKSI

◆ ◆ ◆

This is a glorified bread pudding, a nursery dessert as beloved of Armenian expatriate families as it is of those in the old country. The *kaimak* can also be used as a topping for fruit salads, or eaten on its own with a sprinkling of nuts.

SERVES 6

For the kaimak
◆ *750 ml/1¼ pt double cream* ◆ *425 ml/¾ pt milk*

For the ekmek
◆ *12–15 x 2 cm/¾ in thick slices Greek, sour dough or other country-style bread, crusts removed*
◆ *50 ml/2 fl oz milk* ◆ *30 ml/2 tbsp water*

For the syrup
◆ *450 g/1 lb sugar* ◆ *225 ml/8 fl oz water*

Make the *kaimak* first. In a square or rectangular flameproof casserole or pan with sides at least 5 cm/2 in high, combine the double cream and the milk. Simmer over low heat and scoop out some of the mixture. Lift your arm high over the casserole and let the liquid stream back into the pan.

Continue to scoop and pour the liquid for the next 15 minutes, until the entire surface of the mixture is covered with little bubbles. Lift the pan carefully from the heat, making sure not to agitate it, and move to a warm place. Leave for 2 hours, then move to room temperature for 2 more hours. Then carefully transfer to a refrigerator for 24 hours.

Run a knife around the edges of the pan and cut the top layer of solidified cream into long strips and then into shorter strips. With a spatula, lift the strips off the milk and transfer to a plate. Cover with cling film and chill. (The *kaimak* will keep for about 5–6 days in the refrigerator.)

To make the *ekmek*, preheat the oven to 170°C/325F/Gas Mark 3. Toast the bread slices on a baking tray for 10 minutes, or until they are dried and golden.

Arrange the toasts in a slightly overlapping layer in a baking dish or shallow casserole. Combine the milk with the water and pour the liquid evenly over the toasts. Set aside.

To make the syrup, combine the sugar with the water in a saucepan. Bring the mixture to the boil over high heat, stirring, then lower the heat slightly until it begins to thicken. Then bring to the boil for 1 minute and remove from the heat.

Set the oven to 180°C/350°F/Gas Mark 4. Pour the syrup over the toasts and put the dish in the oven. Bake for 40–45 minutes, or until browned and puffed. Allow to cool to room temperature, then serve with the *kaimak* spooned over the top.

BAKLAVA

◆ ◆ ◆

Armenians are the Viennese of Caucasia – mad about pastries. Perhaps this is because so many Armenians were merchants, and making a sale was traditionally done in a friendly fashion – over tea and cakes. Armenian *baklava*, unlike Turkish versions, are traditionally made in a round pan.

MAKES ABOUT 20

◆ *1 packet phyllo pastry (20 x 30 cm/8 x 12 in)*
◆ *675 g/1½ lb walnuts, chopped*
◆ *1 tsp cinnamon*
◆ *800 g/1¾ lb sugar*
◆ *450 g/1 lb unsalted butter, melted*
◆ *450 ml/¾ pt water*
◆ *30 ml/2 tbsp fresh lemon juice*
◆ *large pinch of cinnamon*
◆ *2 whole cloves*

Ideally, use a round baking tin 28–30 cm/11–12 in in diameter. Unroll the sheets of phyllo pastry, keeping them together, and lay the pan over them. Using a sharp knife or pastry cutter, round off the edges of the long ends. (The width will be too short to trim.) Discard the trimmings and reroll the sheets, covering them with a damp towel to prevent them from becoming brittle.

In a bowl, mix together the walnuts, cinnamon and 100g/4 oz sugar. Take out 3 sheets of the phyllo pastry. Butter the pan generously and place one sheet on the bottom. Brush with the butter and cover with another sheet, laid at right angles across the first so that it extends across the width. Brush with butter and cover with a third sheet, at a slightly different angle. Butter that sheet, then sprinkle over some of the nut mixture. Continue layering the phyllo pastry in this fashion until you have used all the nut mixture, then cover the top with 5–6 sheets of buttered phyllo pastry.

Preheat the oven to 170°C/325°F/Gas Mark 3. Score the pastry into a diamond pattern, without cutting through all the way. Bake for 50 minutes, or until the top is golden and crisp. Remove from the oven.

Make the syrup by combining the remaining sugar, the water, lemon juice, cinnamon and cloves in an enamelled or stainless steel saucepan. Follow the method for making the syrup for Armenian Toasted Bread Pudding with Condensed Cream. Pour the hot syrup over the *baklava* and leave for at least 24 hours so that as much syrup as possible will be absorbed. Cut through the scoring to release the diamond shaped pieces.

MELON AND WALNUT COMPOTE

KOMPOT IZ DYNI I OREKHOV

◆ ◆ ◆

**Versions of this simple dessert are eaten from
Greece through Georgia and Armenia to Uzbekistan.**

SERVES 6–8

◆ 2 small cantaloupe or
honeydew melons, halved,
seeded and cubed

◆ 350 ml/12 fl oz honey
◆ 350 g/12 oz walnuts,
chopped

Place the melon cubes, with any juice, in a bowl. Add the
honey and toss to coat lightly. Stir in the walnuts. Divide the
mixture between individual bowls.

FROM THE STEPPES OF TARTARY
Central Asia and Kazakhstan

———

THE ERSTWHILE SOVIET REPUBLICS OF UZBEKISTAN, KIRGIZSTAN, TAJIKISTAN AND TURKMENIA WERE USUALLY REFERRED TO COLLECTIVELY AS THE CENTRAL ASIAN REPUBLICS UNDER THE OLD ORDER AND WERE GROUPED TOGETHER WITH KAZAKHSTAN BECAUSE OF THEIR SHARED CULTURE AND HISTORY. FOR THIS IS SILK ROAD TERRITORY; ACROSS THESE DESERTS AND STEPPES CAME THE ARMIES OF ALEXANDER, THE HORSEMEN OF GENGHIS KHAN AND TAMERLANE, AND THE CAMEL CARAVANS THAT BROUGHT MARCO POLO TO CHINA. DESPITE THE CHANGES WROUGHT BY THE ECONOMICALLY DRIVEN SUZERAINITY OF THEIR MASTERS IN MOSCOW, THESE STATES ARE STILL HARSH LANDS, WITH SAVAGE EXTREMES OF TEMPERATURE AND TERRAIN.

Despite the harsh climate and terrain, romance can be found in these regions: in the blue-tiled city of Samarkand and the winding mud-brick alleys of Tashkent) both in Uzbekistan; in the permanently snow-capped peaks of the Tien Shan and Pamir ranges that define the perimeters of Tajikistan and Kirgizstan; in the verdant oases punctuating the sandy wastes of Turkmenia; and in the staggering emptiness of Kazakhstan, 1900 km/1180 miles from the Volga to the Chinese border.

This vast area is home to some of the peoples least touched by Sovietization, or indeed by the modern world. The 'indigenous' inhabitants are, in reality, a melting pot of races. Mainly Turkic and Persian stock is leavened with Mongolian, Chinese, Siberian, Arab, Gypsy and tribal strains like the Kazakhs and Kirgiz, varying according to state and local regions. National costumes are everyday wear in many streets; the pervasive Sunni culture means that traditional Muslim generosity and inhibitions are equally observed; old ways of living, trading and farming are followed in the remotest spots.

Conversely, the influx of non-indigenous people, particularly after the mid-1930s, has meant that Muslims are now outnumbered in all the states. Ethnic Russians, Ukrainians, Armenians, Crimean Greeks and Georgian Turks, as well as groups of other East Europeans, rub shoulders with the natives in the markets and bazaars. Expelled to Central Asia by Stalin's purges and encouraged by Khrushchev's incentives, their parents and grandparents founded stable communities which now flourish in this alien soil. However, riots and violent confrontations have erupted in several regions during the last few years, sometimes between rival groups and sometimes against the dominance of ethnic Russians in positions of authority. Only time will tell if these sporadic outbursts will grow into something more serious.

Though the visitor is still struck by the ageless appearance of many of the cities and villages and by the open space, the programmes implemented by the Russian masters have resulted in certain dramatic changes. Camels are fewer, replaced by longhorn cattle. Chemical plants, factories, quarries, and massive irrigation canals disfigure the plains, and in the 'Bayconur cosmodrome' in

Kazakhstani Anatoly Tatarenko is presented with a fragrant loaf of bread at the end of the harvest. His team of farm workers achieved the highest level of productivity in the region.

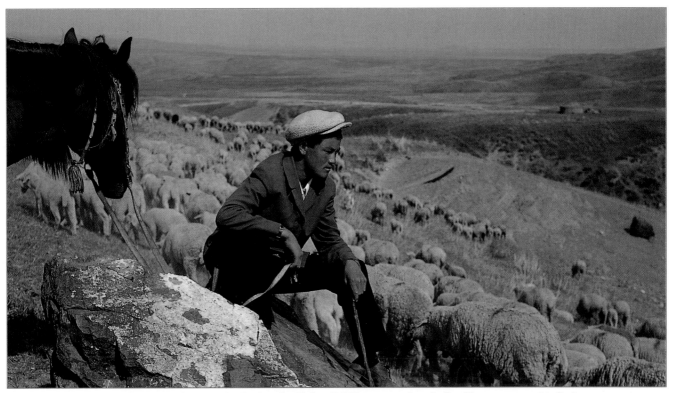

Zhamabek Beisenov, senior shepherd on the Chokan Valikhanov state farm in Kazakhstan, pastures his flock.

Kazakhstan the empty landscape conceals environmental havoc waged by underground nuclear testing. While the channelling of water resources has resulted in a blossoming of once-arid steppeland, the leaden hand of Communist planning has re-created the 19th-century cotton monoculture of the American South, with 20th-century versions of its economic dependency and soil nutrient erosion. Citrus and soft fruits, grapes, melons, dates, carrots, pumpkins, peppers and cucumbers flourish in the land allotted to them, but scattered evidence of ecological exploitation and corruption are unhappily obvious even to the unobservant.

Central Asian cuisine is surprisingly homogeneous, in spite of the huge spread covered by the republics, the range of ethnic groups, and the varying productivity of the land. Its prevailingly Mongol and Tartar origins mean that it is spicy and reliant on bread, rice, yoghurt and lamb. Recently it has become the most fashionable cuisine in the CIS, with several new restaurants opening in Moscow which specialize in it. This is indeed ironic, since in the local hotels and restaurants which cater to foreigners and better-off citizens, it takes second place to mediocre Russian-style cooking.

Uzbekistan has probably given the most recipes to what is generally termed Central Asian cooking; it is the most sophisticated republic, containing the three best-known centres – Tashkent, Samarkand and Bukhara. Their central covered markets (*tsentralny rynok*) and farmers' markets (*kolhoznye rynky*) are a riot of colour in season, and tourists find their senses assailed with a wealth of new sights and smells. Over 1000 types of melon are grown in Uzbekistan alone; only an armful are ever seen in the West.

Plov – rice pilaf made with or without chicken or lamb and enriched with an assortment of fruits and nuts – is a speciality which has variations all over the area. A love of pastries, dumplings and fritters is another characteristic shared by all the states – *manty, chebureki, gutap* and *samsa* are filled with lamb, herbs, eggs, onions or mashed pumpkin (*tykva*), depending on the season and area, while *belyashi* is a particular type of deep-fried meat pasty found in Kazakhstan. *Non* – the flat onion bread – has a name reminiscent of Indian nan, but is in fact more like an Indian paratha in looks, taste and texture.

Another border crossing has brought the Georgian and Armenian delight in walnuts to Central Asia. They can be found in soups, in the pastries offered at the teahouse (*chaikhana*) where, in true Muslim fashion, the men meet to pass the time of day – and in yanchmish, a sticky candy.

The thick meat soups such as *besh barmak* and *mstava* encountered by the tourist in the very basic hotels and cafés are filling but often unappealingly greasy to Western palates. In fact, grease and fat are a hazard of Central Asian cooking, since the sheep raised there are prized not only for their meat but for the quantity of fat rendered from their rumps and tails. In this they bear a striking resemblance to the sheep of the Levant, another instance of cultural cross-fertilization. *Kazy* (horsemeat sausage), *kurt*, a hard and pungent sun-dried ewe's cheese, and *kumys* (fermented mare's milk), found primarily in Kirgizstan and Kazakhstan, are all tastes to be acquired by the seasoned – and gastronomically adventurous – traveller.

CHILLED SALAD SOUP

HOLODNY SUP-SALAT

◆ ◆ ◆

This is an extraordinarily refreshing soup – like a liquid salad. Based on ingredients found all over the Central Republics, it is a refined variation on a common theme.

SERVES 4–6

- ◆ *3 cloves garlic*
- ◆ *4 thick slices Greek or French bread, crusts removed*
- ◆ *50 g/2 oz butter*
- ◆ *2 red onions, thinly sliced*
- ◆ *8 radishes, thinly sliced*
- ◆ *7 large ripe tomatoes, skinned, seeded and chopped*
- ◆ *½ cucumber, peeled and thinly sliced*
- ◆ *salt and freshly ground black pepper*
- ◆ *large dash of Tabasco*
- ◆ *75 ml/5 tbsp vegetable oil*
- ◆ *15 ml/1 tbsp lemon juice*
- ◆ *400 ml/14 fl oz can chicken consommé*
- ◆ *150 ml/5 fl oz Greek- or Bulgarian-style yoghurt*
- ◆ *8 spring onions, finely chopped*

Finely chop two of the garlic cloves and set aside. Use the remaining clove to rub over the bread slices. Roughly cut them into croutons.

Heat the butter in a frying pan and sauté the croutons until golden. Drain and set aside.

In a large bowl, combine the chopped garlic, red onions, radishes, tomatoes, cucumber, seasoning to taste and the Tabasco. In a small bowl, whisk together the oil and lemon juice, then pour over the salad and chill for 1 hour.

Place the chicken consommé in the refrigerator 30 minutes before you make the soup.

Just before serving, add the chilled consommé to the bowl and stir it in thoroughly, then stir in the yoghurt. Sprinkle with the spring onions, and serve the croutons in a separate bowl.

YOGHURT SOUP WITH APRICOTS AND WALNUTS

SUP IZ YOGURTA Z ABRICOSAMI I GRYETSKIMI OREKHAMI

◆ ◆ ◆

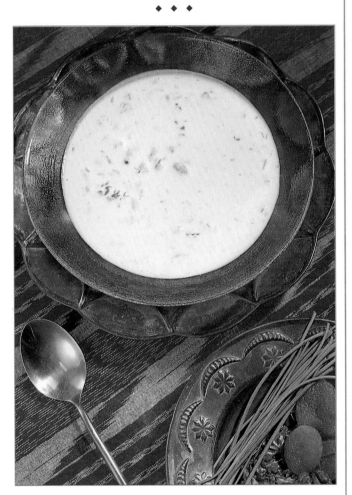

Some of the combinations and textures of Central Asian dishes seem quite strange to Westerners. Dried fruits are ubiquitous, many of which are unknown here; crunchy titbits in smooth cold soups are another surprise.

SERVES 4

- ◆ *450 ml/³/₄ pt Greek- or Bulgarian- style yoghurt*
- ◆ *225 ml/8 fl oz soda water*
- ◆ *50 g/2 oz ready-to-eat dried apricots, chopped*
- ◆ *25 g/1 oz walnuts, chopped*
- ◆ *3 tbsp finely chopped chives*
- ◆ *2 tsp finely chopped fresh dill*
- ◆ *2 tsp finely chopped fresh tarragon*
- ◆ *salt and freshly ground black pepper*

Combine all of the above ingredients in an attractive glass bowl, with seasoning to taste, and stir gently. Chill for 1–2 hours and serve.

RHUBARB TEA

CHAI IZ REVENYA

◆ ◆ ◆

In Uzbekistan and Kazakhstan, rhubarb gleams redly in summer markets. It is eaten raw there, its sour flavour much liked. This sweetened 'tea' is more appealing – and very cooling in the sweltering Asian heat.

MAKES 10–12 CUPS

- ◆ *1.75 kg/4 lb or more fresh rhubarb* ◆ *sugar*
- ◆ *1 lemon, thinly sliced* ◆ *mint leaves*

Wash and drain the rhubarb. Trim off the leaves and tough bottoms of the stalks. Chop the remainder into small pieces. Use a large cup to measure the rhubarb into a large enamelled or stainless steel casserole, counting the number of cups used. Follow with an equal amount of water.

Bring the mixture to the boil over medium–high heat, stirring occasionally. Reduce the heat and cover. Cook, stirring occasionally, until the rhubarb is pulpy.

Strain the cooking liquid into a wide-mouthed pitcher. While hot, stir in sugar to taste – the less sugar the more thirst-quenching it will be. Leave to cool, then chill. Add slices of lemon and a small bunch of mint leaves. Pour into glasses garnished with more mint leaves.

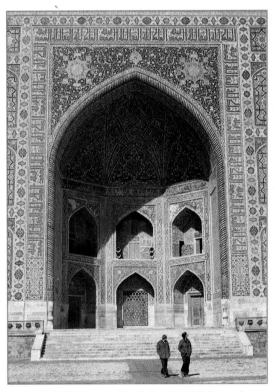

Until the Russian Revolution, the Uzbek city of Samarkand was a centre of Muslim culture, a key staging-post on the Silk Road and, in the 14th century, capital of Mongol ruler Tamerlane's empire.

KAZAKHSTAN LAMB POTATO CAKES
KARTOPHELNYE PIROSHKI Z BARANINOY PO-KAZAKHSKY
◆ ◆ ◆

There are echoes of Afghan and Pakistani cooking in these spicy potato cakes, which resemble *pakhoras*. They would be served with *kumys* (mare's milk yoghurt, though today made commercially with cow's milk) in their native land.

MAKES 12

- ◆ *3 medium-sized red potatoes, peeled*
- ◆ *1 onion*
- ◆ *5 large eggs*
- ◆ *350 g/12 oz lean minced lamb*
- ◆ *3 tbsp plain flour*
- ◆ *1 tbsp finely chopped flat-leaved parsley*
- ◆ *1 tbsp finely chopped coriander*
- ◆ *¼ tsp ground cumin*
- ◆ *salt and freshly ground black pepper*
- ◆ *25 g/1 oz clarified butter*

Grate the potatoes on to a tea towel placed on a work surface. Twist the towel to squeeze out as much liquid as possible from the potatoes. Complete squeezing with your hands, then put the potatoes into a large bowl. Grate the onion into the bowl, and beat in the eggs, one at a time. Stir in the lamb, flour, parsley, coriander, cumin and seasoning to taste.

Melt the butter in a large frying pan over medium-high heat. Add the lamb and potato mixture in amounts of 3–4 tbsp spreading the cakes with the back of a spatula.

Cook until golden-brown, about 6 minutes a side. Drain on absorbent kitchen paper and keep warm until all the cakes have been cooked.

DEEP-FRIED HERB AND EGG ENVELOPES
GUTAP
◆ ◆ ◆

The dividing line between *samsa*, *gutap* and *beliashi* is a slim one, since they are all pastry cases containing many of the same fillings. *Samsas* can be either baked or deep-fried, while *beliashi* are shallow-fried and *gutap* are deep-fried. Here the fresh herbs usual to the latter are enveloped in a melting custard.

MAKES ABOUT 32

- ◆ *8 large eggs*
- ◆ *salt and freshly ground black pepper*
- ◆ *45 g/1½ oz unsalted butter, melted*
- ◆ *1 tsp plain flour*
- ◆ *100 g/4 oz fresh parsley, finely chopped*
- ◆ *50 g/2 oz fresh dill, finely chopped*
- ◆ *25 g/1 oz fresh coriander, finely chopped*
- ◆ *50 g/4 oz kale, finely chopped*
- ◆ *100 g/4 oz spring onions, finely chopped*
- ◆ *vegetable oil*

For the dough
- ◆ *175 g/6 oz plain flour*
- ◆ *150–175 g/5–6 fl oz lukewarm water*
- ◆ *salt*
- ◆ *50 g/2 oz unsalted butter, softened*

Beat the eggs in a large bowl and season to taste. Beat in the melted butter and the flour. Stir in the herbs, kale and spring onions.

Preheat the oven to 180°C/350°F/Gas Mark 4. Butter a baking dish or tin generously and pour in the egg mixture.

Bake in the oven for about 18 minutes, until the custard is just set. Remove from the oven and leave to cool to room temperature.

To make the dough, sift the flour into a bowl and make a well in the centre. Pour in the water, a good pinch of salt and half the butter and, using a plastic spoon or spatula, slowly stir the flour into the wet ingredients until well mixed. Then beat until it becomes a firm dough.

Transfer the dough to a floured surface and divide in half. Cover one half and set aside. Roll the other half into a rectangle, as thin as possible, and fold over once, then over again, until it is four layers thick. Roll out again as thinly as possible, and trim to about 23 x 20 cm/9 x 8 in. Cut the dough into 4 strips lengthways, then divide each strip into 4 equal squares.

Spoon a heaped tsp custard on to each square and draw up the corners to form a packet. Moisten your fingers and pinch the top to seal. Repeat with the remaining 15 or so squares. Cover with a damp cloth and set aside. Roll out the remaining pastry and repeat the process.

Fill a large saucepan or deep-fryer about 10–13 cm/4–5 in deep with oil. Heat until it is very hot (but not smoking) and spits when water is dropped into it (about 190°C/375°F). Fry the *gutap* in 3 batches for about 3–4 minutes each, turning, until they are golden and crisp. Drain on absorbent kitchen paper. Serve warm.

Kazakhstan Lamb Potato Cakes

STEAMED LAMB DUMPLINGS

MANTY

◆ ◆ ◆

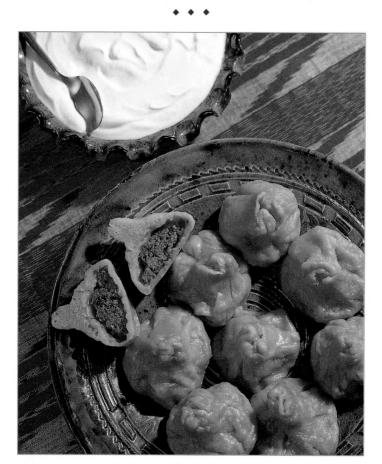

**These are a speciality of Uzbekistan, and bear a
resemblance to Mongolian pot-stickers and similar
Chinese dumplings. The filling is often just minced
lamb, but this version is tastier. *Manty* should be
eaten with the fingers.**

MAKES ABOUT 24

- 675 g/1$^{1}/_{2}$ lb minced
  lean lamb
- 2 small onions, finely
  chopped
- 45 ml/3 tbsp lemon juice
- 50 g/2 oz raisins
- 3 tbsp finely chopped mint
- $^{1}/_{4}$ tsp ground cinnamon
- large pinch of cayenne
  pepper

- salt and freshly ground
  black pepper
- 450 g/1 lb plain flour
- 425 ml/$^{3}/_{4}$ pt water
- butter
- 225 ml/8 fl oz Greek-
  or Bulgarian-style
- yoghurt or 100 ml/4fl oz
  white wine vinegar
  (optional)

In a large bowl, combine all of the ingredients except for the
flour, water, butter and yoghurt or vinegar. Transfer half the
mixture to the bowl of a food processor fitted with the
metal blade. Process until of a pasty consistency. Set aside

and process the remaining mixture. Combine the two meat
mixtures.

Sift the flour into a large bowl. Make a well in the centre
and pour in the water. Turn in the flour and mix thoroughly
to make a smooth dough. Halve the dough, leave one half
covered in the bowl and transfer the rest to a floured surface.
Roll out thinly into a large rectangle.

Using a biscuit cutter or a wide-mouthed jar, cut out
12 cm/4$^{1}/_{2}$ in rounds. Place a scant 2 tbsp filling in the centre
of each dough round. Top each with a dot of butter and pull
up the sides of the dough over the filling to make a small
purse. Moisten your fingers with water, then twist and pinch
the top of each purse to close tightly. Set aside the prepared
manty, covered with a damp cloth, and repeat the process with
the remaining dough and filling.

Add water to a depth of 2.5–5 cm/1–2 in to a large saucepan
and bring it to the boil. Place a steamer or colander over the
boiling water, add half the *manty*, cover, and lower the heat so
the water just simmers. Steam the *manty* for 15 minutes.
Repeat with the remaining *manty*. Serve each batch as soon as
it is cooked, together with a bowl of yoghurt or a small
ramekin of vinegar for dipping, if desired.

STEAK TARTARE

MYASO PO-TATARSKY

◆ ◆ ◆

According to legend, Steak Tartare – the most renowned dish to come out Kazakhstan – was discovered by the fabled horsemen-warriors of Tartary. Always on the warpath, and with little or no time to cook their food, they tenderized meat under their saddles to make it palatable raw. In expensive Russian and East European restaurants, Steak Tartare is always a first course; in the West it is usually served as the entrée.

SERVES 4

- *2 large egg yolks*
- *3 spring onions, finely chopped*
- *10 ml/2 tsp Dijon-style mustard*
- *15 ml/1 tbsp Worcestershire sauce*
- *15 ml/1 tbsp bottled horseradish sauce*
- *15 ml/1 tbsp vegetable oil*
- *10 ml/2 tsp pepper vodka*
- *1 tbsp finely chopped capers*
- *450 g/1 lb fillet of beef, minced three times*
- *salt and freshly ground black pepper*

To garnish

- *watercress sprigs*
- *radishes, trimmed and scrubbed*
- *spring onions, trimmed*

Beat the eggs in a large bowl. One after the other, stir in the onions, mustard, Worcestershire sauce, horseradish, oil, vodka and capers. With your hands, gently work the beef into the mixture, and season to taste. Form into 4 patties and arrange on a serving dish. Garnish attractively with the watercress, radishes and spring onions.

BAKED PASTIES

SAMSA

◆ ◆ ◆

**These baked *samsa* bear a distinct resemblance to
the more northerly *pierogi*, though the spicing is
unmistakeably Asian. They make delicious hors d'oeuvres
for a drinks party – as do all Central Asian pastries,
dumplings and fritters.**

MAKES ABOUT 40

- ◆ 450 g/1 lb lean minced beef
- ◆ 2 small onions, chopped
- ◆ salt and freshly ground black pepper
- ◆ pinch of cayenne pepper
- ◆ 50 g/2 oz fresh parsley, chopped
- ◆ 50 g/2 oz fresh coriander, chopped
- ◆ 45 g/1¹/₂ oz toasted pine nuts

For the dough

- ◆ 225 g/8 oz unsalted butter, softened
- ◆ 225 ml/8 fl oz Greek- or Bulgarian-style yoghurt
- ◆ 275–300 g/10–11 oz plain flour
- ◆ 1 heaped tsp salt
- ◆ 1 egg
- ◆ 15 ml/1 tbsp water

Make the dough first. Cream the butter with the yoghurt in a large bowl. Slowly sift in the flour, a little at a time, beating it in after each addition. Add the salt at the same time. Continue until you have used up all but 1–2 tbsp of the flour. If the dough is still tacky, add as much of the remaining flour as is necessary to make it firm. Cover with cling film and chill for 3–5 hours.

Meanwhile, make the filling. Place the meat, onions, seasoning to taste, cayenne pepper, parsley and coriander in the bowl of a food processor fitted with the metal blade. Process until it is of a pasty consistency. Remove to a bowl and work in the toasted pine-nuts. Chill until needed.

On a floured surface, roll out the dough into a large rectangle. With a biscuit cutter or lid, cut out 7.5–9 cm/3–3¹/₂ in circles. Spoon a heaped tsp filling on each circle, moisten the edges and fold over the dough to make a crescent. Use the prongs of a fork to press and crimp the edges of the crescents. Arrange the pasties on an oiled baking sheet and chill for 30 minutes.

Preheat the oven to 200°C/400°F/Gas Mark 6. Make an egg wash by beating the egg with the water and brush over the pasties. Bake them for about 15 minutes, until golden-brown.

UZBEKISTAN GRILLED QUAIL OR PARTRIDGE

PYEREPYOL ILI KUROPATKA-GRILL PO-UZBEKSKI

◆ ◆ ◆

**Though Uzbekistan is largely desert it also contains
the foothills of the Tian Shan and Alay mountain ranges,
in which can be found plentiful game. Grilled quail and
partridge are a speciality, first marinated in spices
and thick cream**

SERVES 4

- ◆ 8 quail or 4 small partridges, cleaned and gutted, heads removed
- ◆ 90 ml/6 tbsp fresh lemon juice
- ◆ salt and freshly ground black pepper
- ◆ 2 cloves garlic, crushed and finely chopped
- ◆ 2 tsp peeled and grated fresh root ginger
- ◆ ¹/₂ tsp allspice
- ◆ ¹/₂ tsp nutmeg
- ◆ 150 ml/¹/₄ pt double cream
- ◆ vegetable oil

If using partridge, cut them in half. Place the whole quail or halved partridges in a wide bowl and sprinkle with the lemon juice and a heaped tsp salt. Toss and rub the birds with your hands, and leave them to marinate for 1 hour. Then add the remaining ingredients except for the oil, toss, and chill the mixture for 3–4 hours, moving the pieces around once or twice.

Prepare the coals of a barbecue or preheat a grill. On each of four metal skewers, either thread 2 quail or 2 halves of partridge. Truss the birds on, if necessary. Brush the birds with oil and lay them about 10 cm/4 in above the hot coals or under the grill. Cook for about 20–25 minutes, turning once or twice, until the birds are just cooked through and nicely browned. Serve immediately.

Uzbekistan Grilled Quail or Partridge

LEMON-GRILLED LIVER

PYECHEN-GRILL Z LYEMONOM

◆ ◆ ◆

On street corners all over Central Asia, *shashlyk* can be found grilling on portable barbecues, giving off their heady aroma. The most common are variations of lamb kebabs, but offal and chicken versions are also available. Local Muslims would use mutton or lamb fat to moisten their liver but here bacon fat is more accessible.

SERVES 6

- *1.25 kg/3 lb calves' or lambs' liver, cut into 5 cm/2 in cubes*
- *3 medium onions*
- *12 slices streaky bacon*
- *75 g/3 oz butter, melted*
- *60 ml/4 tbsp lemon juice*
- *salt and freshly ground black pepper*
- *lemon quarters, to garnish*

Trim the liver and remove any membrane. Poach the onions in boiling salted water for 5 minutes. Drain and halve each onion; cut each half into 3 wedges. Stretch the bacon over the back of a knife and cut each slice in half. Wrap each piece of liver in bacon.

Thread the bacon-wrapped liver on to 6 long skewers, alternating with 3 onion wedges on each skewer. In a bowl, whisk together the butter and lemon juice.

Prepare the coals of a barbecue or preheat a grill. Brush the liver kebabs with some of the lemon butter, season to taste and cook 7.5–10 cm/3–4 in from the heat, basting occasionally and turning twice. Serve when the liver is browned and crisped on the outside but still pink in the middle, about 10 minutes. Garnish with the lemon quarters.

TURKMENIAN STUFFED PEPPERS

FARSHIROVANNYE PERTSY PO-TURKMENSKY

◆ ◆ ◆

This is a Westernized version of the stuffed peppers one would encounter in Turkmenia. Some of the dried fruits which give it distinction are not to be found here, but this recipe is still redolent of the Silk Road and the East.

SERVES 6

- *6 medium, well-shaped red sweet peppers*
- *15 ml/1 tbsp vegetable oil*
- *675 g/1½ lb minced lean lamb*
- *2 small onions, chopped*
- *225 g/8 oz cooked long-grain white rice*
- *3 tbsp sultanas*
- *45 ml/3 tbsp tomato purée*
- *30 ml/2 tbsp honey*
- *2 eggs, beaten*
- *1 tsp ground allspice*
- *½ tsp ground cumin*
- *½ tsp ground cinnamon*
- *large pinch of cayenne pepper*
- *salt and freshly ground black pepper*
- *225 ml/8 fl oz Greek-or Bulgarian-style yoghurt*

Cut the tops from the peppers and carefully remove the ribs and seeds from the insides. Rinse and drain the shells.

Heat the oil in a large frying pan and add the lamb. Cook over medium heat, breaking up the lamb with a wooden spoon, until the meat is browned. Stir in the onions and cook until they are soft and lightly coloured. Remove the pan from the heat and drain off the fat.

Stir in the rice and sultanas; cook for 2 minutes. Add the tomato purée, honey, eggs and spices; season to taste and combine well.

Preheat the oven to 190°C/375°F/Gas Mark 5. Divide the filling equally between the 6 peppers, pressing it down tightly, and pack them into a shallow casserole. Bake for about 40 minutes, until the tops are browned and the peppers are soft. Serve hot or cold, with a bowl of yoghurt to spoon over.

Lemon-grilled Liver

ALMA-ATA PILAF

ALMA-ATA PLOV

◆ ◆ ◆

There are numerous *plov* recipes originating in Central Asia; this one from the capital of Kazakhstan utilizes the rich bounty of fruit which grow there – the apples are particularly famous.

SERVES 6

- *50 g/2 oz blanched slivered almonds*
- *50 ml/4 tbsp vegetable oil*
- *450 g/1 lb lamb steaks, cubed*
- *2 large carrots, cut into julienne strips*
- *2 large onions, thinly sliced*
- *75 g/3 oz dried apricots, chopped*
- *50 g/2 oz raisins*
- *675 g/1 1/2 lb long-grained white rice*
- *salt and freshly ground black pepper*
- *425 ml/3/4 pt chicken stock*
- *150 ml/1/4 pt orange juice*
- *1 tsp grated orange rind*
- *600 ml/1 pt water*
- *1 medium red apple, cored and chopped*

Preheat the oven to 200°C/400°F/Gas Mark 6. Scatter the almonds on a baking sheet and toast in the oven until golden, about 5 minutes. Set aside and turn the oven down to 180°C/350°F/Gas Mark 4.

Heat the oil in a large frying pan over medium-high heat. When just smoking, add the lamb cubes and sauté for 6 minutes, or until well browned. Transfer the meat with a slotted spoon to a large casserole.

Turn the heat down slightly and sauté the carrots in the oil for 3 minutes, stirring, then add the onions and continue to sauté for another 6 minutes, until the onions are soft and lightly coloured. Stir in the dried apricots, raisins and rice. Cook for 2 minutes until the rice is coated with the oil and is becoming opaque.

Add the rice mixture to the casserole with the meat. Season to taste, then pour over the chicken stock, orange juice and rind, and water. Bring to the boil, then cover the casserole and transfer it to the oven. Bake for 40 minutes, or until all the liquid is absorbed.

Remove the *plov* from the oven, stir in the chopped apple, and transfer it to a large serving dish, making a neat mound. Scatter the toasted almonds over the top and serve.

UZBEKISTAN SWEET WALNUT BRITTLE

SLADKOYE PYECHENYE IZ GRYETSKIKH OREKHOV PO UZBEKSKY

◆ ◆ ◆

**The Central Asians are famous for their sweet tooth –
and for their love of nuts. In this dish the two make a
perfect marriage, bound by the sweetened evaporated
milk common in their desserts.**

MAKES ABOUT 700G / 1 ¹/₂ LB

- ◆ *225 ml/8 oz light brown sugar*
- ◆ *¹/₂ tsp ground cinnamon*
- ◆ *¹/₄ tsp ground allspice*
- ◆ *¹/₄ tsp ground ginger*
- ◆ *75 ml/3 fl oz evaporated milk*
- ◆ *350 g/12 oz walnuts*
- ◆ *¹/₂ tsp vanilla essence*

Place the sugar, cinnamon, allspice, ginger and evaporated milk in a heavy saucepan and stir over high heat for about 5 minutes, or until the sugar dissolves and the mixture reaches soft ball stage (115°C/238°F on a sugar thermometer.)

Remove the pan from the heat and stir in the nuts and vanilla essence. Make sure all the nuts are coated, then pour out on to a sheet of greaseproof paper. Allow to cool, then break into chunks. Store in an airtight container.

WATERMELON ICE

ARBUZNY LYOD

◆ ◆ ◆

The summer months are extremely hot in the arid wastes and teaming towns of Central Asia and Kazakhstan. Vendors sell ices and soft drinks, and while a Western tourist might not risk this watermelon ice on the dusty streets of Tashkent, home-made it is wonderful.

SERVES 4

- ◆ 2.75 kg/6 lb watermelon, rind removed, seeded and cubed
- ◆ 75 g/3 oz caster sugar
- ◆ 175 ml/6 fl oz water
- ◆ 60 ml/4 tbsp lime juice
- ◆ 1 tbsp grated lime rind
- ◆ 1 tbsp very finely chopped mint
- ◆ fresh mint leaves

In a blender or a food processor fitted with the metal blade, process the watermelon pulp until it is a smooth, watery purée. Transfer to a bowl.

In a small saucepan, combine the sugar, water and lime juice and lime rind. Bring to the boil, stirring to dissolve the sugar. Reduce the heat and simmer for 6 minutes, then remove from the heat and stir in the mint. Allow to steep for 2 minutes.

Stir the syrup into the watermelon purée and combine well. Pour the mixture into a plastic or freezing container. Freeze until just firm, then decant into the processor bowl and purée again. Return to the container and freeze until firm. Before serving, allow to stand at room temperature for a few minutes.

SHARON FRUIT SAMARKAND

KHURMA PO-SAMARKANDSKI

◆ ◆ ◆

Sharon fruit, a member of the persimmon family, is named for a region in Israel, but varieties of the fruit itself are found throughout the Middle East and Asia. In Central Asia, they would not include the alcohol – but it does give an extra fillip!

SERVES 6

- ◆ 200 ml/7 fl oz mandarin, tangerine or blood orange juice
- ◆ 1/2 tsp grated orange rind
- ◆ 2 tsp cornflour
- ◆ 15 ml/1 tbsp lemon juice
- ◆ 30 ml/2 tbsp Sabra (Israeli liqueur) or other orange liqueur
- ◆ 6 ripe Sharon fruit or thin-skinned persimmons
- ◆ 4 tbsp pomegranate seeds

Place the fruit juice, rind and cornflour in an enamelled or stainless steel saucepan. Bring to the boil stirring, then continue to stir over high heat until the juice thickens. Remove from the heat and stir in the lemon juice and orange liqueur. Set aside until just warm.

Meanwhile, plunge the fruit in boiling water for 10–15 seconds. Allow to cool then peel, using a sharp knife. Carefully cut the flesh of each Sharon fruit or persimmon into 8 wedges and arrange in a fan shape on 6 dessert plates. Pour the warm sauce over half of each fruit fan and into a pool in the centre of the plate. Scatter the pomegranate seeds over and serve.

DRIED FRUIT AND NUT TART

TORT IZ SUSHYONYKH FRUKTOV I OREKHOV

◆ ◆ ◆

This pastry is inspired by the extraordinary wealth of dried fruits found in the markets of Caucasia and Central Asia. It is chewy, crunchy, melting – and utterly scrumptious.

SERVES 10–12

- ◆ 175 ml/6 fl oz sweet white dessert wine
- ◆ 175 ml/6 fl oz honey
- ◆ 175 g/6 oz ready-to-eat dried apricots or peaches
- ◆ 1/2 tsp grated orange rind
- ◆ 100 g/4 oz blanched whole almonds
- ◆ 3 eggs
- ◆ 5 ml/1 tsp vanilla essence
- ◆ 25 g/1 oz unsalted butter
- ◆ 100 g/4 oz walnuts
- ◆ 225 ml/8 fl oz cream
- ◆ 1/4 tsp cinnamon
- ◆ pinch of sugar

For the pastry

- ◆ 150 g/5 oz plain flour
- ◆ 50 g/2 oz sugar
- ◆ 100 g/4 oz unsalted butter, cut into small pieces
- ◆ pinch of salt
- ◆ 1 large egg yolk

Make the pastry first. Place the flour, sugar, butter, and salt in the bowl of a food processor fitted with the metal blade and process until the mixture has the texture of breadcrumbs. Drop the egg yolk through the tube and continue to process until the pastry forms a ball. Remove and chill for 30 minutes.

Combine half the wine and 25 ml/1 fl oz honey with the dried fruit and orange rind in an enamelled or stainless steel saucepan. Cook over low heat, uncovered, for 20–25 minutes, until the liquid is absorbed and the fruit is puffed and soft.

Meanwhile, preheat the oven to 180°C/350°F/Gas Mark 4. Place the blanched almonds on a baking tray and toast for about 10 minutes, or until the nuts are golden. Remove from the oven. Keep the oven at 180°C.

In a bowl, beat together the eggs, the remaining wine and honey, the vanilla essence and the butter. Beat in the almonds and walnuts. Flatten the pastry with the palm of your hand.

Place in a 250 m/10 in springform tin and press it over the bottom and sides of the tin, pressing it as thinly as possible. Scatter the apricots or peaches over the bottom of the pastry. Pour the egg and nut mixture over the top smoothing evenly. Bake the tart on the middle rack of the oven for 45 minutes, or until golden-brown. Cool in the tin on a wire rack; remove the rim before serving with cream whipped with the cinnamon and sugar.

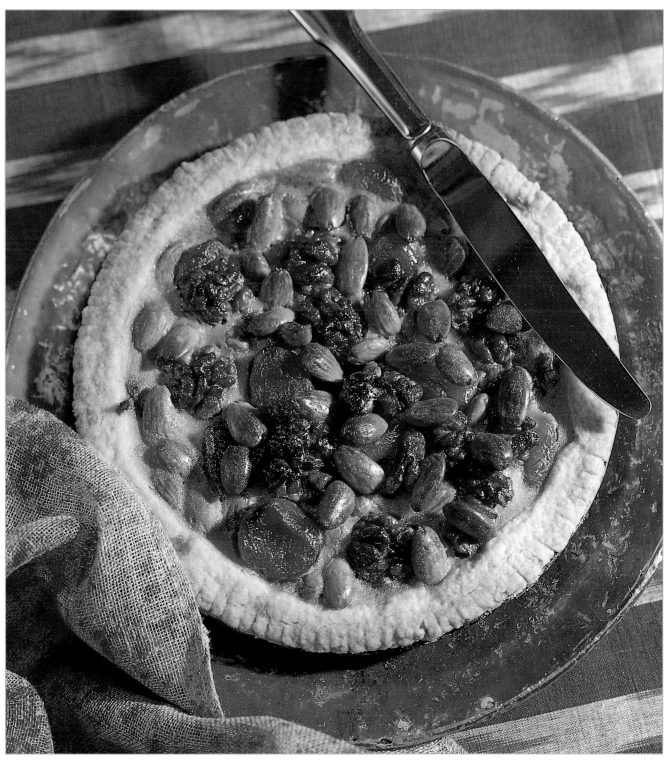

Dried Fruit and Nut Tart

INDEX

◆ ◆ ◆